Since Debussy

A View of
Contemporary Music

André Hodeir

Since Debussy

A View of Contemporary Music

TRANSLATED BY NOEL BURCH

Grove Press, Inc.   •   *New York*

Contents

17848

The first five chapters of this book were originally published in French as part of *La Musique Etrangère Contemporaine* ("Que Sais-je" Series, Presses Universitaires de France) but all have since been thoroughly revised and enlarged. The introduction and conclusion contain passages from the earlier book, but are composed largely of new material. The three chapters that compose Part Two have never before appeared in print; if they seem to constitute more extensive treatments of their subjects than any of those in Part One, this is because the French composers dealt with here are so much less well-known than Stravinsky, Bartók, or the three Viennese (no book, for example, has ever been devoted to the work of Olivier Messiaen).

A word about the translation: in the United States the words "row" and "tone-row" are used to designate Schönberg's invention, called *série* in French and series in England. I have decided to confine my use of the word "row" and its compounds (row system, row composition, etc.) to the original twelve-tone system as it was conceived and practiced by Schönberg, his pupils and disciples, but shall employ the adjective "serial" when referring to the extension of the row concept to other musical parameters, developed since the war by Pierre Boulez and other composers of his generation.

I wish to thank Mark Goodman and Elliot Stein for their helpful suggestions and Eugene Kurtz for his indispensable technical advice.

NOEL BURCH

To readers aware of the complexities peculiar to our age, the title of this book and the intentions it implies may seem over-ambitious. Indeed, it may seem almost presumptuous to publish a book which, in order to achieve its purpose, would require an author thoroughly conversant with every major activity and achievement of our time, not only in the arts but in all other fields of human endeavor. It has always been exceedingly difficult to separate the wheat from the chaff in any collection of recent works. This difficulty is ten times greater in our century, when, depending upon one's frame of reference, music seems either on the verge of extinction or, on the contrary, ready to embark on an unknown but highly promising future. My feeling is that even tomorrow's historians will have trouble unraveling the tangled threads of our period; I can hardly hope, then, to present a clear, all-inclusive picture of it in this book. Still, the attempt is worth making, and I am prompted to do so less by the hope of succeeding than by the feeling that a gap remains to be filled. Even the faintest glimmer of light shed on this subject cannot be superfluous, since music is a source of such confusion for nearly everyone today.

This confusion exists from the very outset, affecting even the realm of generalities. Given the complexity of contemporary artistic idioms and the considerable progress of modern artists in the field of aesthetic sensibility—both related to the "speeding-up of history"—one is readily tempted to reject the achievements of modern art *in toto* without bothering to assimilate them, and to take refuge instead in the most insignificant forms of art, the meager content of which has been pilfered from the past. Now there is an ill-defined yet implacable law governing the relationships between art and history: it is always possible to determine the date, exact to within a few years, of any given work, provided it is truly representative of its period, because that work holds a unique position in a process of historical connections. Those who still doubt the immutability of this process and think that an "inspired" composer could write another *Tristan and Isolde* or *Jupiter Symphony* are deluding themselves so completely, that this book can be of no possible use to them.

Introduction

Music and Civilization

If we carry our respect for the past too far, we are in danger of detaching ourselves from the present, and this error can be aggravated by a misconception of the humanistic attitude. Although college students painstakingly explore vast expanses of the past, they are brought up short on the very threshold of the contemporary world; nor do they always pursue their studies on their own and examine the world around them for its deeper meanings. In this respect, the general public is even more underprivileged. Everyone is so anxious to please the masses that no one takes the trouble to educate them. Nothing—or next to nothing—has been done to span the gulf between the artist and the average man, with the result that the average man prefers the path of least resistance: content with Mozart and Chopin he feels no need to seek out the masterpieces of his own day and is not even aware of his ignorance. A few people, of course—

and not all of them snobs—do derive pleasure from certain scores they think are modern, and hail them as masterpieces; they are entirely unaware that these works are only superficially modern and that they are applauding the Meyerbeers of their day.

Every word of what I have just written would have been equally pertinent at the turn of the century. The famous "divorce" between the artist and his public was perfectly apparent then; in fact, it has been so ever since Beethoven's day. Nevertheless, a situation which is perfectly normal in itself can, in exceptional circumstances, acquire special meaning. Since 1945, the phrase "the atomic age" has been on everyone's lips, but a deeper truth may well lurk behind this facile cliché. The convulsions that wrack our civilization today may be the symptoms of its impending death, but they may also foretoken the birth of a new world.[1] If the second hypothesis is correct, then the groundwork for an authentically new art form must already have been laid somewhere. For art is more than the mere reflection of an age, it is its very soul; yet the truth of the matter is that very few composers have had a *feeling* for this age of ours, hence the prevailing state of confusion on the subject of "modern music." But, of course, the problems raised by twentieth-century music may simply be more acute and agonizing than those man has had to face in the past.

In the light of contemporary history, the lag of approximately forty years separating the average man from the artist acquires an almost tragic significance. I am reminded of that character in an Orson Welles film who stumbles into a Chinese theater and for whom the actors' frenzied behavior appears as

---

[1] Other writers are setting forth similar speculations. In his introduction to the vast *Encyclopédie de la Pléiade*, Raymond Queneau writes: "The increasing utilization of cybernetics, the conquest of atomic energy, and the fact that Asian and colonial peoples now have access to both social and individual autonomy are three of the most recent reasons for Western man to feel that he is standing on the threshold of a new era."

the absurd expression of an utterly incomprehensible universe. The public—and I mean the cultivated public—may be just as puzzled by contemporary art; languages have come into existence which may be completely meaningless to the average spectator. Perhaps the above mentioned gap has been replaced by a wall, beyond which lies a new civilization. Perhaps the twentieth-century artist no longer belongs to the same world as his contemporaries. The great historian Arnold Toynbee believes that the growth of civilizations is due to the creative acts of certain minorities, but also to the mimetic faculties of the masses. Right now, there is reason to doubt that these faculties are being fully exercised. In this period of transition between two civilizations, that mighty, creative vanguard composed of philosophers, scientists, and artists seems to be having difficulty inducing our contemporaries to fall in behind it.

The Transitional Role of the Years Between the Two World Wars

If it is true that we are living in a pivotal period, that we are witnessing the death throes of an age-old art and the birth of new forms of thought and sensibility, then we should not be surprised to find our age conspicuously lacking in the plethora of musical masterpieces which marked the great classical periods. It seems undeniable that the period from 1918 to 1945 was richer in promising scores than in polished masterpieces. The reasons behind this slump are fairly clear. In the first place, less music is being written now than in the past; the problems facing the individual composer have become so complex that the existence of a Vivaldi, who, in Luigi Dallapiccola's words, wrote not six hundred concertos but the same concerto six hundred times, would be inconceivable today. In the second place, composers have lost their placid self-confidence. By the end of the first World War, the great tonal tradition, which had already been greatly shaken by Debussy and undermined by Schönberg, was too weak to sustain any great music, while the new language, which was still being painstakingly elaborated, was neither sufficiently rich nor well organized as yet to produce music of a breadth and cohesiveness comparable to the great works of the past. The twenties and thirties, with their many apparently conflicting tendencies, were essentially periods of experimentation. Every work of art is, naturally, an experiment in itself; but an experiment based upon a firmly established tradition and a fully developed idiom does not have the agonizing, speculative character of a number of those carried out between 1920 and 1940 by artists who were awakening to a new conception of music. This is the sense in which it has been suggested that music is about to enter a second Middle Ages, and that the great composers of our time bear a closer resemblance to Perotinus and Machaut than to Mozart or Bach.

Does this mean that we should ignore contemporary music altogether and scorn the first half of the twentieth century as a period of utter decadence and nothing more? This attitude—unfortunately all too prevalent—is a sign of intellectual cowardice. A period which, in the brief span of thirty years, has brought forth four or five musical geniuses and a great many talented composers, which has seen the growth of so many new concepts and laid the groundwork for a complete reorganization of the musical universe, is of undeniable importance. Furthermore, the twentieth century does not always suffer by comparison with other periods in musical history. If we consider the period bounded by the death of Mozart on the one hand and that of Beethoven on the other, a period comparable in length to that which we are discussing, we have to admit that it was not exactly teeming with musical geniuses. Of course, Stravinsky, Schönberg, Messiaen, and their fellows have often met with failure. They may have only glimpsed the wonders which their successors will one day achieve—are, in fact, already achieving. Yet whether their task was to add a few last stones to the tonal structure, or whether they struck out to explore the future, their contributions are inestimable. They were destined by their historical situation to play the difficult role of intermediaries; posterity will no doubt pay tribute to them insofar as each carried out the task allotted him by his fellow men without betraying his individual genius.

The Myth of Independent National Schools

An objective examination of the facts may or may not corroborate the thesis that we are passing from one civilization to another, and that this step will bring about a basic transformation in European art. But first, we must determine the best vantage point from which to conduct this examination. How can we best appraise contemporary music? Should it be examined as a whole, or can it be better grasped by attempting to define and then distinguish between conflicting tendencies?

At first glance, one of the most convenient ways to attack the problem might seem to be in terms of the so-called national schools. Everyone is familiar with the musical repercussions of that epidemic of nationalism which spread across Europe in the wake of the Napoleonic Wars. The "national schools of music" that sprang out of that typically nineteenth-century movement have lasted well into the twentieth. Never had there been so much talk of composers "with" or "without" passports as in the twenties and thirties of the present century, at a time, that is, when we were gradually realizing that we were all Europeans and when the phenomenon was beginning to subside.

Even today, however, many talented composers still employ material borrowed from their country's folklore. This sentimental attachment to a tradition that is decaying in its own right—how many Western countries can still boast of an authentic, living folk music in this radio-conscious age?—is, in itself, no mean indication that a major epoch of European art is on its way out. For it is a far cry from the way Bach used a popular air in the *Goldberg Variations* to the way certain contemporary composers use folk tunes as oxygen tents. Furthermore, the turmoil resulting from the second World War and its antecedents did a great deal to disrupt national schools. Paul Hindemith's influence is now far greater in the United States than in his native Germany, while young Austrian musicians have only just discovered the three great Viennese composers (Schönberg, Berg, and Webern; they were banned by the Nazis), through the recent teachings of a few disciples who had long been prevented from proselytizing.

Thus, it should be clear that a fair appraisal of contemporary music in terms of national schools is quite impossible. It seems to me that the best way to shed adequate light on twentieth-century music is to treat each major composer separately, attempting to show the course of his development and the nature of his contribution. This method may seem overly fragmentary, but then Western music in the twentieth century differs from the music of the past precisely by its widely divergent tendencies and individual experiments. This method also implies a choice on my part, one which I shall eventually have to justify. Many readers may be surprised to find that I devote entire chapters to composers who are infinitely less well-known than others who are hardly discussed—Olivier Messiaen rather than Arthur Honegger, Jean Barraqué rather than Sergei Prokofiev. But my choice was based on very strong musical convictions, which are, I feel, rigorously motivated. And in any case I like to hope that my arguments, although they cannot, of course, change anyone's mind—only the music itself is capable of that—will at least have the merit of drawing the reader's attention to certain aspects of modern music the importance of which he may, in part, have overlooked.

A Tribute to Claude Debussy

It may also seem a pity that a book claiming to deal with modern music and its outstanding masters does not begin with a chapter on Claude Debussy. I have not made this omission for fear of attacking widespread opinions. It is generally agreed, of course, that the first notes of the *Prelude to the Afternoon of a Faun* brought about a far-reaching upheaval in musical sensibility, and that they marked the beginning of modern music. But the deeper implications of Debussy's music and its historical significance were not brought to light until the end of the last war. Only then did "Claude de France," the "soft-focus painter," the "impressionist," and "pointillist" give way to the real Debussy, the composer who destroyed rhetoric, invented the contemporary approach to form, and reinstated the power of pure sound, sound *per se*. We have come to realize that Debussy was both the Van Gogh and the Cézanne, the Rimbaud and the Mallarmé of music. Three centuries earlier, Claudio Monteverdi had played a role which was identical to Debussy's, except for the fact that the musical history which he disrupted had not yet produced the *Clavierübung* Organ Mass, the *Magic Flute*, or the Fourteenth Quartet. "Monteverdi," writes Claudio Sartori in the sedate Larousse Dictionary, "was the last madrigal-writer and the first opera-composer. However, this definition must not be taken as a strict historical fact. People went on writing madrigals long after Monteverdi. . . . But Monteverdi is the composer who marked the end of a kind of music which was henceforth regarded as inadequate to the aesthetic conceptions and the spirit of the period." Similarly, Debussy marked *the end of the symphony* insofar as his works carried deep within them a means of transcending the large-scale forms devised and developed by the classical and romantic masters. Independently of any stylistic problem, his work constituted an irrevocable condemnation of all the Sibeliuses and d'Indys among his contemporaries, as well as of the Shostakoviches and Honeggers to come. Those who, like Igor Stravinsky, tried to recreate a symphonic music derived from the forms of the past were simply "putting on wigs" and "thinking like eighteenth-century composers," as Georges Auric has recently admitted. Debussy is to be hailed as the first musician to have had the courage to adopt twentieth-century thought processes, thereby making inevitable the disappearance of old habits which the so-called neoclassicists of the twenties and thirties vainly sought to revive. Recent criticism has confirmed this view; I have in mind especially the analytical studies by Jean Barraqué, the composer. In fact, my decision not to discuss Debussy was prompted by the fact that Barraqué, for whose genius I have the greatest admiration and respect, is now finishing an essay on Debussy which is, I feel, of major importance. I have had access to his book, and anything I could write on the subject would be, in the main, a mere rehashing of its contents. The reader will understand why I feel reluctant to infringe upon an essay of this sort prior to its publication. The composer of the *Nocturnes* will not, however, be omitted from this book completely, for his shadow spreads over all of contemporary music, and especially the most recent. Even when he is not actually mentioned by name, the presence of Debussy will be felt on every page through the influence of his splendid music.

Part One

There is a French proverb which says *A tout seigneur tout honneur;* its rough English equivalent is "Honor to whom honor is due." In the eyes of the general public the *seigneur*—or lord—of contemporary music to whom all honor is due is Igor Stravinsky, the most brilliant, the most capricious, and without doubt the most famous composer of our time. I need hardly add that, despite the almost universal enthusiasm for his work, I am not one of his wholehearted supporters, and am, in fact, surprised at the general opinion that the composer of that masterpiece *The Rite of Spring* can do no wrong. I feel it would be almost indecent to refer to him in the same breath with Debussy. I also feel that there are other great men less fortunate than he—especially Anton Webern, the composer whom Stravinsky most admires—who equally deserved success and recognition during their lifetimes and the material and spiritual comfort that go with them. Lastly, I find very disturbing the social phenomenon which has shockingly allowed Stravinsky's fame to outlive his creative genius by a good many years.

Stravinsky was fortunate enough to write his masterpiece at the age of thirty and to have come in contact with a good many influential minds determined to impose it on the public. Proust once wrote that "the time . . . that a person requires . . . to penetrate a work of any depth is merely an epitome, a symbol one might say, of the years . . . that must elapse before the public can begin to cherish a masterpiece which is really new," but he went on to add that "the work itself . . . , by fecundating those few minds capable of understanding it, will cause them to grow and multiply . . . marking in this way, like every great work of art, an advance . . . in intellectual society, largely composed today of what was not to be found when the work first appeared, that is to say of persons capable of enjoying it."

If these assertions are correct, then it is not surprising that a *violently* novel work like *The Rite of Spring*, which was, moreover, "launched" with a good deal of ballyhoo, should have made *its* way with unprecedented rapidity, and brought such fame to the young composer that his name was soon well-known even to the general public. The lack of discrimination shown by this same general public with regard to Stravinsky's later works, the reverence dictated by a reflex of blind confidence, is hardly less surprising.

Our century, which has promoted so many kinds of dilettantism, needed a Great Dilettante. This, I feel, is the most accurate description of Igor Stravinsky, even at his most "ascetic"; the stylist in him has devoured the artist.

CHAPTER ONE

Igor Stravinsky

Stravinsky's Career

Igor Stravinsky was born on June 17, 1882, in Oranienbaum, near Saint Petersburg, where his father sang at the Imperial Opera. He began studying the piano when he was nine, but his first real musical training was autodidactic, and he spent most of his free time after school reading scores. At the University of Saint Petersburg he made friends with the son of Rimski-Korsakov, who introduced him to his father. Between 1906 and 1908, while studying orchestration with the composer of *Sadko*, Stravinsky wrote his First Symphony and an orchestral fantasia called *Fireworks*.

In 1909, Stravinsky met Sergei Diaghilev, the impresario of

the Ballets Russes, who was impressed by the promise contained in *Fireworks* and commissioned the young composer to do a ballet based on an old Slavic legend; this was to be *The Firebird*. The ballet's première, held the next year at the Paris Opera with choreography by Fokine, was so successful that Stravinsky instantly became a leading figure in Western musical circles. With three consecutive works, all written for Paris performances of the Ballets Russes—*The Firebird* was followed by *Petrouchka* (1910-1911) and *The Rite of Spring* (1912-1913) —Stravinsky quickly proved that he was the most brilliant composer of his generation. During this period, Stravinsky lived partly on the Atlantic coast of Europe, partly in Switzerland, and partly in Oustiloug, his private estate in Russia. On May 29, 1913, Pierre Monteux conducted the world première of *The Rite of Spring* (choreography by Nijinsky) at the Théâtre des Champs Élysées in Paris; this date was to go down in musical history. The novelty and aggressiveness of the work created an unprecedented scandal.

A few months before the war, Stravinsky settled in French Switzerland; he lived there for six years, during which he completed his opera *The Nightingale* (1908–1914) as well as a symphonic suite called *The Song of the Nightingale* (1917) which was drawn from it. He also wrote the Three Pieces for String Quartet, *Pribautki* (1914), *Renard* (1916–1917), *L'Histoire du Soldat*, *Ragtime* (1918), *Pulcinella* (1919), and did the first sketches for *Les Noces*. The October Revolution placed him in a difficult position. Deprived of the income from his estate, he found himself obliged to support himself and his family. *L'Histoire du Soldat*, written in collaboration with C. F. Ramuz, and *Pulcinella*, commissioned by Diaghilev, were both occasional works.

In the last weeks of 1919, Stravinsky left Switzerland and went to settle in France, residing alternately in Nice, Biarritz, and the Paris suburbs. He then wrote the *Symphonies of Wind Instruments* (1920, dedicated to the memory of Debussy), did a piano transcription of *Petrouchka*, and completed *Les Noces* (1917–1923). An *opéra bouffe, Mavra* (1921), the Octet for Wind Instruments (1922–1923), and two piano works—the Concerto (1923–1924) and the Sonata (1924)—were followed by two ballets, *Apollon Musagète* (1927–1928), and *Le Baiser de la Fée* (1928), then by a third piano work, the *Capriccio* (1929). He also composed the opera-oratorio *Oedipus Rex* (1926–1927), on a libretto by Jean Cocteau. During this same period, much of his time was spent touring the principle cities of Europe and even America, for he was somewhat pressed for money and had taken to giving performances of his own works, either from the conductor's podium or at the piano.

In 1930, Stravinsky first tried his hand at religious music with his *Symphony of Psalms* for chorus and orchestra, commissioned by the Boston Symphony Orchestra. The following year, Stravinsky left Nice and went to stay in the Alps, there writing the Violin Concerto and, in 1932, the Duo Concertant for violin and piano, both for Samuel Dushkin. Then came the cantata *Perséphone* (1933–1934) on a text by André Gide, followed by the *Divertimento* (1934) and the Concerto for Two Solo Pianos (1935), which had its world première with Stravinsky and his son, Soulima, at the keyboards. *Jeu de Cartes* (1936), a ballet in three "deals," the *Dumbarton Oaks Concerto* (1937–1938), and the *Symphony in C* are the last works of his "French period."

Stravinsky, as it happened, was in the United States when war was declared. He settled in Hollywood, gave up his French nationality (acquired after the Russian revolution), and became a naturalized American citizen. He now completed the *Symphony in C* (1938–1940) and re-orchestrated *The Firebird, Petrouchka*, and *The Rite of Spring*. Some of the major works which he has written in the United States are the *Danses Concertantes* for chamber orchestra, (1941–1942), the *Four Norwegian Moods* (1942), and the *Ode* (1943), both for orchestra, the cantata *Babel, Scènes de Ballet* (1944), the Sym-

phony in Three Movements (1945), the Concerto for Strings
(1946), the ballet *Orpheus* (1947), the Mass (1948), the opera
The Rake's Progress (1950), and the Cantata on Elizabethan
lyrics (1952). It was in this last named work that Stravinsky
first made use of the tone-row technique, which became increasingly prevalent in the works that followed: the Septet (1953),
the *Canticum Sacrum ad Honorem Sancti Marci Nominis*
(1955), *Agon* (1954–1957), and *Threni* (1958). His conver-
sion to the "reviled" doctrine caused great consternation among
his admirers. A number of minor scores, such as the *Scherzo à
la Russe* (1944), written for Paul Whiteman, the *Ebony Concerto*, dedicated to Woody Herman's jazz band, plus chamber
works such as the Two-Piano Sonata (1943–1944) and the
Elegy for viola (1944), round out the vast and highly varied
catalogue of Stravinsky's works.

There is hardly a domain of composition left untouched by
Stravinsky in the course of a musical career which has already
covered half a century. Though his works have never ceased
to be controversial, the composer of *The Rite of Spring* may
be considered a fortunate man. Except for a few years of hard-
ship following the Russian revolution, he has had the rare good
fortune of being able to live by his pen, and in greater luxury
than most composers have ever known. The première of *The
Rake's Progress* at the Venice Biennale of 1951, hailed as a
major event by journalists the world over, was probably the
high point of prestige in the career of a composer who, already
famous at thirty, has since become, along with Pablo Picasso,
the most pampered artist of our time.

The Supreme Musical Achievements:
The Rite of Spring *and* Les Noces

It is generally felt that Stravinsky's musical career proper began with *The Firebird*. External influences are, of course, often
apparent in this score; some passages might well have been
penned by Rimski-Korsakov or Debussy. But its best pages

rise far above mere slavish imitation; the "Prelude," with its breathless figure-work in the wood winds and its passages of silence, added a new shade to the impressionist palette, and "Katchei's Dance" owes nothing to the rather facile orientalism of *Sadko*. This early work revealed an important facet of Stravinsky's genius: his remarkable feeling for the possibilities of the modern orchestra. Taking the orchestrations of Rimski-Korsakov—which summed up all the past achievements in this domain—as a springboard, and profiting by the more recent discoveries of Debussy and Ravel, Stravinsky was preparing to revolutionize orchestral technique.

The promise contained in *The Firebird* was brilliantly fulfilled in Stravinsky's next work, *Petrouchka*. It is amazing that a composer under thirty should have attained such mastery of a technique in which imagination does not easily compensate for inexperience. And yet, perfect though it was, his orchestration was even more remarkable for its originality. By doing away with pedal-point, Stravinsky freed the orchestra from the influence of the organ. He also introduced the notion of "pure sonority," conceived independently of the musical context. The clarinet part, for example, is written as a function of the instrument's specific qualities rather than simply as a melodic line. But though relieved of its purely musical burden, the orchestra remains closely associated with it, continuing to convey the over-all character of the work. The orchestral effect suggesting an enormous accordion is often cited as an example of musical "realism," while the snatch of a Dranem song that follows was considered another "shocking" device.

The extraordinary crescendo-like progress of Stravinsky's music between 1910 and 1913 reached its climax with *The Rite of Spring* which was, poetically, far superior even to *Petrouchka*. The work is full of uncanny orchestral effects which would be quite disturbing to the ear were they not part of an over-all scheme of carefully balanced contrasts. When the repressed tension of the "Introduction," predominantly scored for wood winds, suddenly gives way to the brutal, sledge-hammer rhythms of the strings introducing "Spring Rounds," the effect produced is truly brilliant. Similarly, in the "Introduction to Part Two," the halo of sound obtained by combining muted strings with harmonics in the flutes and double basses, furtively joined by the soprano clarinet, constitutes a long range preparation for the explosive "Dance to the Glorified One."

From a "morphological" standpoint, *The Rite of Spring* is not nearly so complex nor so revolutionary as was first believed. It has been considered a sort of apotheosis of polytonal writing, but this, I feel, is a tendentious interpretation of the score. There are a few major-minor contrasts, but these actually tend toward polymodality rather than polytonality, just as the occasional superposition of several different chords merely results in the formation of modes rather than in any dual tonality. Nor does the novelty of the work lie in Stravinsky's handling of polyphony. In this respect, it might even be considered a step backward; as Pierre Boulez has observed, *The Rite of Spring* is "coarsely written." Most of the time, thick clusters of sound move about in groups, and there is no apparent concern for the continuity of the middle parts. At times, the polyphonic writing congeals into motionless, or nearly motionless verticality. Obviously, this is not what makes the work so remarkable; its deeper significance lies elsewhere.

Even the least knowledgeable listener immediately realizes that the basic innovation of *The Rite of Spring* has to do with rhythm. But it was a good many years before anyone was able to define the exact nature of this innovation. Credit for the first lucid analysis of the work must go to Olivier Messiaen. Previous critics had only praised the great variety and expressive power of the shifting rhythms employed by Stravinsky. It was left to Messiaen to grasp their full implications. He pointed out the existence of "rhythmic characters," figures which develop, expand and contract, behaving in short like living creatures. Using this concept as a point of departure, an essay by Pierre Boulez, carefully buttressed with examples, shows how these rhythmic cells evolve according to highly rigorous patterns. Boulez also demonstrates, using only simple arithmetic relationships, that *The Rite of Spring* offers the first example in Western music since Machaut and Dufay of an *essentially rhythmic language.*

It is hard to summarize the notions brought to light in Boulez's analysis. Two main principles, however, seem to govern the language of *The Rite of Spring.* First of all, Stravinsky gave

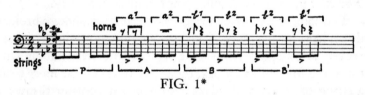

FIG. 1*

The accented theme in "Spring Rounds" as analyzed by Pierre Boulez: P: preparation. A: rhythmic cell (made up of two elements: a^1 and a^2). B: second rhythmic cell (b^1 and b^2). B': obtained by inverting the components of B. The development of the entire section is based on this rhythmic theme.

new meaning to both rhythm and melody *per se* by establishing structural relationships of reciprocity between them. Secondly, he evolved a concept of rhythm based on the notion of *asymmetrical balance.* One can detect the existence in *The Rite of Spring* of *rhythmic themes* which, at times, shuttle back and forth between the melodic line and its accompaniment (e.g., the "accent-theme" in "Spring Rounds") (Fig. 1). By permutating and inverting the order of its component cells, a given theme can be made to provide an astonishingly complex range of rhythmic variations (e.g., "Sacrificial Dance"). A conflict between two types of rhythmic forces—rhythmic structures versus simple rhythms—can be the basis for one type of development (e.g., "Dance of the Abduction"), while other types are evolved by combining several moving rhythmic cells contrapuntally (e.g., "Dance to the Glorified One"), or by establishing oppositions between structures derived either from horizontal dissociations and vertical associations or from mono-rhythmic—or polyrhythmic—organizations of the musical material (e.g., "Dance to the Earth," "Sacrificial Dance"). Still another type of development, predominant throughout most of the "Introduction," involves a kind of "tiling process," or *gradual overlapping*. Each of these techniques was a contribution of revolutionary importance; they are what made *The Rite of Spring* a turning point in musical history.

The components of a work of this perfection, though broken down here for purposes of analysis, are of course tightly interwoven. Although rhythm is the principal and determining factor in the form of this work, the orchestration is far more than a string of gratuitously dazzling effects; it actually throws a powerful light on the work's foundations. Even the written texture, despite its massiveness—or perhaps because of it—plays a clarifying role and contributes to the poetic vitality of the work as a whole.

Once this shattering masterpiece was completed, Stravinsky seemed to mark time, even though the best music he turned out during the war years would have sufficed to make a good many other composers famous for life. In *Renard* he did not always carry to its logical conclusion the dialectical approach to rhythm inaugurated in *The Rite of Spring;* but he did discover a few new, attractive aspects of poetic expression in music. Many passages of *The Nightingale* display a remarkable flair for non-tonal melody, reminiscent of Schönberg's *Pierrot Lunaire* (the same influence had already been felt in a minor work contemporary with *The Rite of Spring: The Japanese Lyrics*). This was but a passing tendency with Stravinsky, however, who now became, on the contrary, increasingly concerned with reviving diatonicism.

Les Noces is a strange work indeed; it is part cantata, and part ballet, since each character is interpreted by a singer *and* a dancer. Chorus and soloists are accompanied by an instrumental ensemble whose composition was thoroughly original for its time: four pianos, tympani, xylophone, bells, tambourine, triangle, crotalum, cymbals, and bass drum. This all-percussion ensemble—even the pianos are treated percussively—may be considered a Westernized version of the Balinese *gamelan* orchestra. It serves to "embellish" with more complex rhythmic patterns the simple rhythmic figures stated by the singers. For not only does *Les Noces* resemble *The Rite of Spring* in that rhythm is its basic component, but Stravinsky's handling of it is similar in both works. The vocal style of *Les Noces* is highly distinctive; its choppy, triphammer delivery is designed to stress syllabic values rather than to convey the somewhat naive poetry of a text inspired by Russian folklore. Short note values play a large part in the work's rhythmic construction. Eighth notes, in particular, are used a great deal, and their frequent repetition on a single note (or on two alternating notes) has an obsessive effect. The highly simplified melodic line lends itself admirably to this treatment. It contains no developments whatsoever, in the accepted sense of the word, but tends, on the contrary, toward a kind of static equilibrium. The melody is composed of snatches of folk or pseudo-folk songs, and is of a very fragmentary nature; its developments consist only in the persistent repetition of a single figure—occasionally in distorted form—or in the juxtaposition of two complementary figures; less frequently, a melodic figure is subjected to a very simple form of variation-development.

The vocal writing makes only sparing use of the extremely high and low registers. On the other hand, abundant—though sober—use is made of ornaments. The over-all coloring of the work is modal, and any ambiguity on this count is dispelled by forceful polarizations; the pivotal note in the "First Tableau," for instance, is E, the point of convergence for all the harmonic and melodic figures.

Though the intrinsic perfection of this work is beyond dispute, it is not so great nor, above all, so original, as *The Rite of Spring*. Indeed, the priority of rhythm over melody is not their only common trait. The two works have other, more subtle organic relationships, for, despite a few touches of humor and a certain atmosphere of jubilation, that same anti-lyricism and incantatory spirit which were so explosively revealed in *The Rite of Spring*, also pervade *Les Noces*. In fact, this "second draft," so basically similar to though less powerful than the first, would be regarded as Stravinsky's masterpiece, were it not for *The Rite of Spring*. The full implications of this observation become clear in the light of the composer's later development, when each new work was supposed to be "a fresh start." The fact that Stravinsky, though continually looking for new worlds to conquer, has never again achieved anything so lovely as this "remake" of *The Rite of Spring*, would seem to prove that in the earlier work he was on the right track.

The Decline and Fall of Stravinsky

With *L'Histoire du Soldat, Ragtime,* and *Pulcinella,* Stravinsky embarked upon a form of expression which was soon to dominate all his music: the stylistic exercise. He had apparently come to look upon composition as a game of skill, and one at which he particularly excelled. *L'Histoire du Soldat,* in particular, might have been written by some circus juggler turned composer; in it Stravinsky accomplished a genuine *tour de force.* The work is a sort of musical cocktail containing, helter-skelter, a fake tango, a mock ragtime, a sarcastic two-step, a sublimated czardas, and a discordant chorale, but the total effect is one of extraordinary unity. This miracle of virtuoso writing was made necessary by Stravinsky's original choice of seven apparently ill-assorted instruments: violin, contrabass, clarinet, bassoon, cornet, trombone, and percussion.

The chorales "à la Bach" in *L'Histoire du Soldat* marked the first appearance in Stravinsky's music of two tendencies which were to prevail in all his subsequent work. The first was that notorious "revival" of the classical forms and styles which had such an inexplicable vogue among French, and to a lesser degree, Western composers between the two World Wars. The second tendency was purely aesthetic and, though apparently in contradiction with the first, was actually its indispensable complement: it was a musical equivalent of that pictorial masochism inaugurated by Picasso at about the same time (though less powerful and authentic than its visual counterpart). More than one artist of the period began dredging the depths of ugliness, hoping to come up with some new form of beauty. The grating dissonances in the *Petit* and *Grand Chorals* were a first step in this direction, but *Ragtime* went much further. In this work, which was, in a certain sense, far less successful than *L'Histoire du Soldat*,[1] Stravinsky seemed to wallow in a voluptuousness of horror. A bit later, the *Symphonies of Wind Instruments* constituted a further apologia for ugliness in sound, this time however in a more discreet and static form. The same features recur in a work of Stravinsky's later years, the Mass.

These two tendencies were synthesized in *Pulcinella* and a whole series of disconcerting works written during the twenties. *Pulcinella* is a perfect example of the stylistic exercise; it is an orchestral suite based on themes by Pergolesi which Stravinsky set about "modernizing" both melodically and harmonically. The specious nature of such an undertaking is self-evident. The brusque intrusion of dissonances in a consonant framework shocks the sensitive ear and reveals the astonishing fact that the "magician" is capable of serious lapses in taste. But the aesthetic concepts involved in this so-called return to Bach

---

[1] See my examination of the "influence" of jazz on European music in *Jazz: Its Evolution and Essence* (Grove Press, New York, 1956). I believe I have shown that this so-called influence was in fact much less important than many critics seem to feel.

held many more disappointments in store. Stravinsky was gradually losing his rhythmic zest and displayed an increasing relish for barren harmony and stilted melody; even the bright hues of his orchestral palette began to fade. Some say that the wizard was turning ascetic. A strange kind of asceticism indeed! The *Octet, Apollon Musagète*, and the piano music belonged to a new variety of academic music which was no better than the old. Stravinsky reached a new high in sheer boredom, however, with *Oedipus Rex*. This interminable score was a paradoxical compound of pompousness and poverty; one has the impression that a piece of hackwork by some Versailles court composer has been exhumed and garnished by a malicious gremlin with aesthetically indefensible dissonances—or rather discords.

This period, which was only feebly enhanced by two minor satirical pieces—the Suites for orchestra—did nevertheless end with an important work: the *Symphony of Psalms*. This score is an undeniable success aesthetically, though many listeners, insensitive to its aura of mystery, unjustly rank it with the music that immediately preceded it. For a time it allowed one to hope that after the painstaking experimentation of the twenties, Stravinsky had at last found a new style. Though the *Symphony of Psalms* is first cousin to *Oedipus Rex*, the two works are worlds apart, in a way, however, which is difficult to define. We might say that the *Symphony* differs from *Oedipus Rex* as a glacier does from a desert. Is this because the work was Stravinsky's first attempt at spiritual music? Did this fresh challenge reveal a hitherto unsuspected side of his genius? Whatever the case may be, and though the *Symphony of Psalms* is no doubt an accident in its composer's career, two of its three movements—the central fugue is not of the same caliber—do constitute, with their curious, static style, an effort to express disincarnate myth. Although this goal is never quite attained, the attempt might have provided food for thought for the aesthetician. More substantial and authentically modern splendors have, however, since appeared upon the scene. This work may actually have been music's final, heart-rending farewell to sacred art.

In any case, the *Symphony of Psalms* remains an isolated phenomenon in Stravinsky's output between the two World Wars. *Jeu de Cartes* is a dull, lifeless score, and in the *Symphony in C* he seems actually to have derived pleasure from piling one cliché on top of the next; the work might almost be a parody on Saint-Saëns. With the *Dumbarton Oaks Concerto*, "patterned" after the *Third Brandenburg Concerto*, he stooped to the lowest form of neoclassicism. Among later works, the Symphony in Three Movements is hardly worth mentioning, the *Scènes de Ballet* are little better than the worst Tchaikovsky, and the Mass is simply caricatural. *The Rake's Progress* was an attempt to revive eighteenth-century opera by a transfusion of "modern" elements, but, despite the care with which the vocal parts were written, it was a final confirmation of Igor Stravinsky's decline as an artist. Stripped of the picturesque qualities which made *L'Histoire du Soldat* worth listening to, the stylistic exercise, no matter how clever it may be, cannot delude exacting music lovers.

The Stravinsky Riddle

Most of Stravinsky's neoclassical works were attempts to create a new musical synthesis by absorbing the most heterogeneous elements in Western musical tradition. This may be why direct or implied quotations crop up so often in these scores, whose melodic facility, reminiscent of the eighteenth-century Italians, is curiously hampered by a stilted, ceremonial approach. Is Alexandre Tansman right when he implies that Stravinsky feels justified in appropriating music which is, after all, in the public domain, and in transmuting borrowed elements into personal traits? Such a procedure hardly seems very authentic. A composer who copies the development of a piece of music from a borrowed pattern—even borrowed from a masterpiece—is simply confessing his inability to renew a form of composition.

Similarly, a composer who grafts dissonant harmonies onto a conventional melody has merely found an easy way to elude the problems of musical language. Considering the insignificance of the works on which Stravinsky squandered his talents trying to work out this retrogressive, contradictory synthesis, it is sad to think back upon that mighty artist who, at the turn of the century, devised a revolutionary approach to the problems of rhythm in music. As a matter of fact, Stravinsky's adoption, at the age of seventy, of the one guiding principle he had shunned until then—the tone-row—could be interpreted as an implicit disavowal of his past development. Of course, the music which the aging master has written more or less in accordance with the row technique is hardly more convincing than that which preceded it. The composer of *The Rite of Spring* has come to the row too late in life either to assimilate it properly or to find in it an authentic extension of his own musical sensibility. The attempt was doomed to failure from the very start. It is all very well for die-hard Stravinsky enthusiasts to maintain that the tone-row technique in the *Canticum Sacrum* derives from a "personal" conception of the row; the fact remains that those "*vocalises byzantines*," as Pierre Boulez calls them, which bind the twelve notes together in a kind of medieval *cantus firmus*, cannot be taken seriously.

The sporadic character of Stravinsky's career is precisely what prevents his being pegged into any of the generally accepted categories. Though at times his music was frankly of the "light classical variety," its elegance preserved it even then from vulgarity, and this is not the easiest thing in the world to achieve. *L'Histoire du Soldat* has fostered a tremendous quantity of similar music, almost all of which is absolutely nil. A great many composers were only too happy to seize upon the master's example and use it to cover their own puny ambitions. But we need only compare *L'Histoire du Soldat* with this or that ballet of recent years to realize the distance that can separate two works with similar aims. Nor does Stravinsky's music belong to any "expressive" school, even though he is one of the greatest of all illustrators of literary and choreographic themes. His attitude is diametrically opposed to the romantic one, for in denying music's power to express any human feeling whatsoever, Stravinsky implies the existence of entirely new values that lie outside the range of emotional expression, and which may well constitute the basis for the music of the future. Stravinsky's music breaks with tradition most effectively, perhaps, by its "magical" qualities. The rhythmic idiom of *The Rite of Spring*, the horizontal and vertical rigidity and repetitious figures associated with it, are the concrete expression of an ecstatic incantation.

Even in the light of such a brief examination, the creative development of Igor Stravinsky appears as an astonishing, and even disturbing phenomenon. To solve the Stravinsky riddle would require absolute insight into his character; but Stravinsky's character is disconcerting and elusive. How could a man who had written a masterpiece as convincing as *The Rite of Spring* stoop to signing scores like the Concerto for Strings, or *Scènes des Ballet?* Is he a prankster at heart—and even, at times, a parodist—or did the genius who composed *Les Noces* simply resign himself to doing stylistic exercises because he found himself in a creative impasse?

Various answers to these questions have been put forth in attempts to shed light on Stravinsky's career. I cannot agree with Mr. Tansman, for example, who maintains that Stravinsky's music is still as good as ever; this viewpoint, which holds that the Symphony in Three Movements is a logical outgrowth of *The Rite of Spring* and its innovations, seems prompted by friendship rather than lucid analysis. Jean Barraqué, on the other hand, has debunked the foolish but widespread notion that Stravinsky has done what film-composers do, adapting his music to each new subject as it came along. "This viewpoint," writes Barraqué, "would make even *The Rite of Spring* seem no more than a brilliant joke. The acceptance of such an explanation would soon lead to the conclusion that artistic creation is a form of witchcraft and nothing more." Pierre Boulez asserts that although the weak points in the scoring of *The Rite of Spring* were at the origin of Stravinsky's rhythmic discoveries, they soon took precedence over those discoveries and finally inhibited their development. He goes on to add that "logically speaking, Stravinsky could not be content with such a hasty system, patched together with a lot of composite, anarchic recipes. He found immediate, hypnotic relief in a return to the tried and true musical hierarchy, tinged with eclecticism." Finally, there are still other, more spiteful observers who claim that having risen to fame at an early age, Stravinsky was simply out to "get rich quick."

I, however, feel that Stravinsky is one of those exceptional creators who, because they are born during the last stages of a civilization, must necessarily hasten its downfall. Having made the tremendous effort necessary to attain the outermost limits of an artistic tradition, having actually burst them asunder, these creative destroyers are probably destined to retrace their steps once more and spend the rest of their lives rehashing the work of their predecessors, like the wave that strikes the cliff just once, then washes out to sea again, losing its identity forever. We shall find this same ebb and flow in the careers of other great contemporary composers.

Be that as it may, however, it is possible—and even probable—that from posterity's broader viewpoint, the outlines of Stravinsky's work as a whole will gradually fade away, leaving *The Rite of Spring* to shine alone as one of the masterpieces of contemporary music.

The history of Western music has been a gradual triumph of artifice. The discovery of *equal temperament* at the beginning of the eighteenth century was one of man's least trumpeted yet most astounding victories over nature. For thousands of years he had been singing and playing instruments in accordance with the natural laws of resonance. The original five-note scale developed into a seven-note scale and later, in certain civilizations, attempts were made to handle a chromatic scale, based on the half tone (the Greeks are even supposed to have used the quarter tone). But the men who devised these scales were still trying to respect natural phenomena; their unevenly tempered whole tones and half tones still belonged to a hierarchy governed by two privileged intervals: the fifth and the octave. Each scale had the dominant as its pole of attraction and rested upon an immutable foundation, the tonic. But European polyphonists were already busy elaborating that miracle of artificiality, the tonal system—which contained such a splendid challenge to nature in the minor mode—and the requirements of their craft soon led them to take a first, all-important step toward freedom. By agreeing to divide the octave into twelve strictly equal half tones, the composers of Bach's day made a decisive break with the natural order of things. In thus transcending the natural limits of musical discourse, they opened the way, not only for the most eminently "human" works of art in history—*The Saint Matthew Passion* and Beethoven's Ninth Symphony—but for the most abstract, as well—*The Art of the Fugue* and the finale of the *Hammerklavier Sonata*. These works, born of the marriage between the tonal system and the concept of equal temperament, were far more beautiful than any previous music, and perhaps than any previous work of art.

There is no reason to shrink from the truth: this Faustian pact with artificiality is responsible for the incomparable grandeur of Western music. The invention of equal temperament was only half the battle, however. Polyphony was to reach an even more crucial turning point when composers found themselves obliged to do away with all the natural elements still remaining in the tonal conception. For tonal music carried within itself the very principle that finally caused its death: chromaticism. The day was to come when musical discourse as such would founder on the shoals of an ever shifting chromaticism and stray, once and for all, from the course of tonal unity. Then, the sense of tonic attraction would cease to exist, the notion of discourse itself would vanish, and rhetoric would be replaced by a dialectic. Eventually, polyphony was to reach a stage in its development when the octave, the natural resonance *par excellence*, would no longer be considered "pure." This step, however, could not be taken gratuitously; it had to be the logical end result of successive stages in the development of polyphony. Yet once polyphonic writing did become so deeply rooted in dissonance as to banish even the octave, it was the sign that artificiality had been so completely mastered that new and greater masterpieces could be envisaged.

That day came when music had lost faith in itself and was passing through one of the dimmest periods in its history, for it was in the years that followed the first World War that the three great Viennese composers accomplished their revolution, offering an unexpected and fertile solution to the problem: the twelve-tone row.

CHAPTER TWO

Arnold Schönberg

Schönberg's Career

Arnold Schönberg was born in Vienna on September 13, 1874. His parents died when he was only eight, and his childhood was rather difficult. He first came to music three or four years later when he took up the violin. He is said to have written little duets, trios, and quartets, to be played by himself and his school-mates. Egon Wellesz, his biographer, stresses the importance of this early contact with chamber music. The young Schön-berg began studying composition by himself, and the only lessons he ever received were a few classes in counterpoint with Alexander von Zemlinsky, when he was twenty-two. The first public performance of a number of *lieder* from his opuses 1, 2, and 3 was given in 1898, with Zemlinsky at the piano. The music created a small scandal, "and the scandal has continued ever since," as Schönberg once good-naturedly declared.

In order to earn his living, Schönberg had to ply all sorts of trades, notably that of bank clerk. In 1901 he married Mathilda von Zemlinsky and the couple moved to Berlin, where for a while he conducted a music hall orchestra; he also went on to orchestrate a good many operettas. Prior to his marriage, he had completed his first major work: *Verklärte Nacht*, op. 4, for string sextet (1899). In 1900 he begun his huge *Gurrelieder*, a kind of enormous cantata which took him eleven years to complete. Among the other works composed in and around his thirtieth year are the symphonic poem *Pelleas and Melisande*, op. 5 (1902–1903), the Songs, op. 6 and 8, the D Minor Quartet, op. 7 (1904–1905), the Chamber Symphony, op. 9, Two Songs, op. 14 (1907), and the Quartet in F Sharp minor, op. 10 (1907–1908).

It was around that time that Schönberg first became known outside of *avant-garde* circles. His financial situation was still so precarious, however, that he made several—unsuccessful—bids at prizes in musical competitions; the Two Ballads, op. 12 and a choral piece, op. 13 were written for this purpose. But his songs were being sung fairly regularly and the Rosé Quartet had added his opus 7 to its repertory, devoting no less than forty rehearsals to it. Though his outspoken notions on music met with hostility in almost every quarter, a group of young people did come to him for lessons. His teaching activities were to prove extremely fruitful, for among the pupils whom he wrapped in an almost despotic care were Alban Berg and Anton Webern, two of the greatest composers of our time.

From 1908 until the beginning of the first World War, Schönberg was creatively very active. He finished orchestrating *Gurrelieder*, wrote a long *Theory of Harmony*, and composed some of his most famous music: Songs from *The Book of the Hanging Gardens*, op. 15, based on poems by Stefan George (1908), Five Pieces for Orchestra, op. 16 (1909), the "monodrama" *Erwartung*, op. 17 (written in the space of two weeks, in September, 1909, just before his thirty-fifth birthday), *Die glückliche Hand*, op. 18 (1909–1913), another one-act lyric drama, for which he himself wrote the libretto, Six Little Pieces for piano, op. 19 (1911), and finally, his masterpiece, *Pierrot Lunaire*, op. 21 (1912). During this period he began to acquire international renown and was asked to conduct his works in Amsterdam, Saint Petersburg, and London. At the same time, his friendship with Richard Strauss enabled him to obtain a professorship at the Stern Conservatory in Berlin, as well as the Franz Liszt Award.

Schönberg was first mobilized in 1915 and finally released from the army in October, 1917. That same year he founded his Seminary for Composition in Vienna. At that time the composer of *Pierrot Lunaire* seemed about to devote the rest of his life to teaching; he even taught for a few months in Amsterdam. Those years of silence came to an end with a discovery which was to have incalculable repercussions: that of the twelve-tone row system. The Piano Pieces, op. 23 (1923), which marked his return to composition, contain the first music—a waltz—composed according to the new technique. There followed the Serenade, op. 24 (1923), the Suite for piano, op. 25, the Quintet for Wind Instruments, op. 26 (1924), the Pieces, op. 27 and Satires, op. 28, both for mixed chorus (1925), the Septet, op. 29, the Third Quartet, op. 30 (1926), and the Variations for Orchestra, op. 31 (1927–1928). In 1929 Schönberg wrote a one-act comic opera, *Von Heute auf Morgen*, op. 32. His last works written in Europe were Musical Accompaniment to a Film Scene, op. 34, Six Choral Pieces, op. 35 (1930), and two Pieces for piano, op. 33 (1932). The opera *Moses and Aaron*, which dates from the same period, was never completed. In 1925, Schönberg had replaced Busoni as professor at the Prussian Academy of Fine Arts in Berlin, but was obliged to resign only a few weeks after the rise of Hitler and, when nearly sixty, left Europe for the United States.

He first taught at the Malkin Conservatory in Boston and then, in 1936, accepted a professorship in composition at the University of California at Los Angeles. There he finished his Second Chamber Symphony, op. 38 (begun in 1906), and also composed his last works: the Concerto for Violin, op. 36 (1936), the Fourth Quartet, op. 37 (1937), the *Kol Nidre* cantata, op. 39 (1938), the Organ Variations, op. 40 (1940), the *Ode to Napoleon*, op. 41, the Concerto for Piano, op. 42 (1942), the Theme and Variations for Wind Band, op. 43 (1944), the Prelude, op. 44 (1946), the *String Trio*, op. 45, *A Survivor from Warsaw*, op. 46 (1947), the Fantasy for violin and piano, op. 47 (1949), the Songs, op. 49 and, lastly, op. 50, the tryptich which includes two *a cappella* choral works—*Dreimal tausend Jahre* and a setting of the 130th Psalm—and the *Modern Psalm* for speaker, chorus and orchestra. He also intended to finish his oratorio *Jacob's Ladder*, begun in 1913.

Arnold Schönberg died in Los Angeles on July 13, 1951. He had been an American citizen since 1940. His friend and pupil, Max Deutsch, has spoken of him in these moving terms: "A readiness to hear, to listen to those who came to him, the look of grave eyes that encourage, that promise friendship: four generations of disciples and friends have known this strange power which raised them above themselves." Schönberg, who had been converted to Catholicism after the first World War, reverted to Judaism in 1933, as a token of solidarity with persecuted Jewry. Schönberg did not lead an easy life. His firm and lofty character earned him bitter enemies. He often railed and chaffed against "conservatory hacks." His witticisms were ferocious and revealing; in reply to a critic who deplored the excessive "modernity" of his works, he said: "My music is not modern, it is just badly played!" Hollywood once sent someone to ask him to do the music for a film. Schönberg set such a high fee on his services that the producer was taken aback and let the matter drop. When his pupils, who knew that their teacher was poor, expressed surprise at his failing to take better advantage of the opportunity, Schönberg gave them this admirable answer: "When you sell your soul to the Devil, you must sell it for a very high price!" He always followed the path he felt was his, not without a certain arrogance, but brooking no compromise. And though he had taught himself everything he knew, he showed real concern for the education of budding composers, writing four very important educational treatises.

Schönberg's Work: 1) Elimination of the Tonal System

With Schönberg's music, as with Stravinsky's—their careers ran curiously parallel—we may adopt a chronological approach. Until 1905, Schönberg merely seemed to be one among many composers who were perpetuating nineteenth-century Germanic traditions. The morbid ecstasy of *Verklärte Nacht* and the bombast of *Gurrelieder* reveal the strong influence of decadent romanticism on this young enthusiast of Wagner and Mahler. Schönberg never rid himself completely of this influence, and we must bear it in mind if we wish to understand his later development. But while most of his contemporaries never went beyond an aesthetic conception which had already been superseded by Debussy's *Pelleas*, it was to Schönberg's credit that he carried this conception to its utmost limits.

Technically speaking, this first stage of his development coincided with the gradual abandonment of the tonal system. Almost imperceptibly, Schönberg moved from a Wagnerian chromaticism—still delimited by the tonal framework—to pure chromaticism. This development was fairly similar to De-

bussy's, who had already attempted—though less systematically, of course—to "drown tonality" in certain interludes of
Pelleas. With Schönberg, this intention became increasingly
clear with each new work, from the Chamber Symphony, op.
9, to *Pierrot Lunaire*, op. 21. Despite its harmonies built on
fourths, the tonal fabric of the Chamber Symphony is still quite
obvious, by comparison with the drastic atonality of *Pierrot
Lunaire*. But the Chamber Symphony did contain one very important innovation: the linear expression of a harmonic figure
(in this case it was a chord of fourths that gave birth to a theme);
this idea was later developed into a compositional technique
based on the rational manipulation of the interval.

Schönberg's development in the early nineteen-hundreds
was not confined to this particular aspect of polyphony. Not
only did he give counterpoint a new lease on life, as it were,
but he also invented a new approach to orchestration. The
Chamber Symphony, though aesthetically a minor work, constituted, historically speaking, a healthy, double-barreled reaction against the two main forms of post-romantic gigantism.
In contrast with Bruckner's endless symphonies and their huge,
compact orchestral apparatus, Schönberg offered the short, con-
cise development of a work which condensed the usual four
movements into one and, by individualizing instrumental tone-
color, offered a more rigorous solution to the problems raised
by the modern orchestra. This "chamber orchestra style,"
though ill-defined as yet, was to have brilliant descendants. The
Five Pieces for Orchestra, op. 16, was a masterpiece of orchestration in which Schönberg perfected the aesthetic concepts introduced in the Chamber Symphony. In this work, he
displayed an entirely new approach to scoring for large orchestra. The instrumental variations on a single chord in the
third Piece—"Summer Morning by a Lake; Colors"—beto-
kened an extraordinarily acute aural sensitivity and brought to
light a new concept: the *Klangfarbenmelodie*, or "melody of
tone-colors." Here, tone-color became the main dimension of

a music whose harmonic and melodic ingredients were deliberately minimized. In the fifth Piece, "The Obligato Recitative," this notion assumes an entirely different form: the *Klangfarbenmelodie* is woven into a marvelous counterpoint in which each melodic line is carried by a constantly alternating succession of the various instruments (Fig. 2).

Of course, this was still no more than a large-scale instrumental *coloring* of polyphony; in Schönberg's opus 16, the role of the *Klangfarbenmelodie* was expressive rather than structural, the work's actual form still being determined by a classical-

FIG. 2*

romantic type of rhetoric which divides musical discourse into phrases. This conventional equilibrium, however, was merely an outward one, for two powerfully destructive agents were at work, undermining the very foundations of music. Discarding the conjunct motion dear to the classicists and pre-Wagnerian romantics, Schönberg began to make systematic use of the hitherto rarely used disjunct interval, incorporating it in his polyphony. Though this concept did promote a kind of hyper-lyricism in the melodic line it also gave rise to contrapuntal conflicts which in turn created a permanent sense of tension. On the harmonic level, the same goal was achieved by different means; the suspension of tonal functions and the systematic rejection of consonance were a second source of steady high tension. Thus, the notion of alternating tension and relaxation, which was the basis of all classical music, had been seriously challenged. These two contributions of Schönberg's —the exploration of disjunct intervals and of non-tonality— were unquestionably of great importance, but they were constantly on the verge of being nullified by Schönberg's fondness for the traditional idea of "pre-existing" musical forms. A daring approach to musical idiom on the one hand, and a certain meekness towards his spiritual ancestors on the other, constituted the two poles of the contradiction from which Schönberg never escaped. Even the Viennese master's most exciting music already contained the seeds of his ultimate failure.

Erwartung was Schönberg's first attempt at opera. He must have been greatly attracted by the possibilities for concentrated expression afforded by this one-character drama in which a woman, waiting for her lover in a forest, finally stumbles upon his dead body. In *Erwartung*, which lasts less than half an hour, Schönberg boldly did away with the usual operatic paraphernalia; not only did he use no leitmotifs, but he carried the concept of "perpetual melody" to its farthest logical conclusion, completely eliminating repetition. Schönberg was standing at the gates of a musical world from which the very notion of theme is excluded, but he was not yet equipped to cross the threshold, and was never to approach it again. The vocal part, sustained by a magnificent orchestration, often rises to dizzy heights of exacerbated lyricism, diametrically opposed to the *bel canto* style. The emotional power and weird poetry of this music-drama make it the undeniable forerunner of another expressionist opera, Alban Berg's masterpiece, *Wozzeck*.

The Six Little Pieces, op. 19, were conceived in the same spirit of extreme condensation. In this work, Schönberg may have been influenced by his former pupil, Anton Webern, whose predilection for "the small form" will be discussed in a later chapter. This type of work, which automatically excludes redundancy of any kind, provides an especially favorable medium in which to develop an absolute-variation form.

While Stravinsky was composing his masterpiece, *The Rite*

of Spring, Schönberg completed *Pierrot Lunaire,* aesthetically his finest work. After having mastered the modern orchestra, Schönberg now went on to prove that he could excel in the composition of chamber music, with a work which represents a compromise between the *lieder* cycle and the cantata. Five instruments—flute, clarinet, violin, 'cello and piano—weave about the solo voice a fabric whose texture varies with each of the twenty-one pieces that go to make up the score. In one piece, the flute plays unaccompanied, in another the 'cello converses alone with the piano; the violinist may, at times, exchange his instrument for a viola, or the clarinetist take up a bass-clarinet. Needless to say, Schönberg handled the various registers of each instrument with consummate virtuosity and, despite the small number of instruments used, he managed to create a climate of extraordinarily varied sonority.

However, it was Schönberg's handling of the human voice in *Pierrot Lunaire* that most astounded music-lovers of the period and made him notorious overnight. In this work, he made systematic use of the *Sprechgesang,* or inflected speech technique, first experimented with in *Gurrelieder.* This "spoken melody" provided a solution to the problem of lyrical declamation, for it both emphasized the contours of the German language and participated in the musical context. The singer's voice indicated the pitch of each note instead of actually singing it, and immediately slid up or down to the next note. This expressionistic technique fitted perfectly into Schönberg's aesthetic concepts at that period, which combined a sense of sobriety with an extreme form of lyricism.

"Morphologically" speaking, *Pierrot Lunaire* summed up all the achievements of Schönberg's "second period" (which extends from opus 6 to opus 22). By now the tonal system had been entirely eliminated; *Pierrot Lunaire* contained not the slightest reference to either a tonic or a dominant. But once the musical language is deprived of its very bases, how can it be organized? The answer lies in an arrangement of melodic and harmonic figures based upon a limited number of *intervals*. Thus "Nacht," the eighth piece in *Pierrot Lunaire*, considered one of the most perfect examples of precursory tone-row composition, is built entirely on a three-note motif—E, G, E-flat. This motif is transposed, inverted, retrograded, written out as a melody or built up into a chord, so as to provide the basis for a passacaglia-like development whose multiple contrapuntal ramifications are derived from a material which was extremely simple at the outset. Schönberg attained an equally high degree of intellectual complexity in other passages, such as the eighteenth piece, in which two simultaneous canons—one for piccolo and clarinet and another for violin and 'cello—are each written in strict retrograde movement (a technique used by Beethoven in the *Hammerklavier Sonata*).

And yet somehow, this architecture seemed to lack a unifying principle. Schönberg had found it impossible to make progress without drawing all the logical conclusions from that tendency toward pure chromaticism which had increasingly dominated Western music since Wagner; this implied the destruction of the very basis of that music, tonality itself. How, and with what, was he to replace the solid foundation hitherto provided by the attraction of the tonic and the hierarchy of key-relationships? Was it enough merely to do away with these forces of attraction? Perhaps they ought to be reinstated? On the eve of his fortieth birthday, these were the questions puzzling that extraordinary creator who had just challenged all the laws on which European music had thrived for centuries. A long period of meditative silence was about to begin for Schönberg.

Schönberg's Work: 2) *The Invention of the Row*

As we have already seen, he did not break this silence until he felt he had solved the problem. The solution he offered was the *twelve-tone row*. In elaborating the tone row principle, Schönberg made his first constructive contribution to music, for the row made it possible to organize the "chaos of atonality" along rational lines.

The row system is based upon a new approach to the chromatic scale, that is to the twelve distinct notes which our Western ear, owing to its musical conditioning, chooses to distinguish, ignoring intervals of less than half a tone. The tonal system of music treated certain notes preferentially, thereby setting up hierarchical relationships. The twelve-tone row system proclaims that all notes are equal (this was already implicit in non-tonality, since no note had the power to attract any other note), but the row's chief function is to establish order. Once the twelve notes have been arranged in a given sequence, the entire work (or fragment of a work conceived as an entity) will necessarily derive from this *row*, from its eleven possible transpositions on the various degrees of the chromatic scale, or from its inverted, retrograde, and retrograde-inverted forms. Thus, in the course of the work as a whole, the generating idea —which by itself is neither a theme nor a mode—may assume as many as forty-eight different forms without affecting the fundamental unity of the musical discourse. Within a given constituent cell, none of the twelve notes which go to make up the row may be sounded twice until all the eleven others have been heard; this is to avoid "polarizing" the melody, or harmony, as the case may be.

The retrograde and inverted forms are of tremendous importance in row composition, which was conceived essentially as a tool for exploring all the possible aspects of a single musical idea, thus submitting it to a continual process of variation. A series of notes, considered at several different points within a given work, may never be exactly identical and never entirely different. The row composer considers that an absolute identity exists between a given interval, its octave, and its inversion. If, in the original row, a D-sharp is followed by a B, these two notes may be presented in a great variety of forms: as an ascending sixth, thirteenth, or twenty-seventh; or as a descending seventeenth or third. Thus, the original order in which the composer arranges his twelve notes becomes the keystone of the entire work, since the row determines *the limits within which it may evolve.*

Clearly, the evolutionary process begun in 1905 had finally resulted in a considerable shifting of musical functions. The preponderant role of "good" harmonic degrees, the power of attraction exerted by certain notes upon certain others, and the relationships between different keys, all notions upon which the tonal universe had been predicated, lost their meaning once that universe itself had ceased to exist. At first, it was the *interval* which, as we have seen, played the basic functional role in the embryonic world of non-tonality. Then another shift occurred, and this role fell to the order in which the intervals were arranged, and consequently to the order of the notes which formed them.

The row was not merely a consequence of Schönberg's concept of absolute-variation; it was actually a crystallization of all the various contributions involved in non-tonal music. Of these, the most important is undoubtedly *the identity established between the vertical and the horizontal.* A melodic figure derived from the row can be converted into a harmonic figure, and vice versa. Thus, in Schönberg's conception, the row provides both the thematic material and the elements of the secondary parts.

Schönberg soon began to build up large-scale themes involving several periods, each of which utilized the same row in a different form. In his excellent analysis of Schönberg's most important row composition, the Variations for Orchestra, op. 31, René Leibowitz has demonstrated that each of the four periods which make up the theme derives from a different aspect of the same row (Fig. 3). The initial melodic material is provided by the row in its original form (Fig. 3, measures 34–38). In the second period (measures 39–45) the row appears in its retrograde inversion, transposed down a minor third. In the third period (46–50) the melodic line is the strict retrograde of the original row. In the fourth, which bears certain rhythmic relationships with the first, the row is again transposed down a minor third, but here it is merely the inversion, not the retrograde, which is used (51–57). This last period, which is, in a sense, a close variation on the first, is accompanied (from measure 52 on) by a counter-melody which is another transposition

FIG. 3*

of the row and whose first four notes are a partial rhythmic diminution of the theme's initial figure.

The melodic unity obtained in this way is strengthened by a deeper kind of unity, in which melody and harmony are conceived as one. As Mr. Leibowitz points out, the harmonization of the theme in Schönberg's Variations is "merely a vertical projection of the horizontal components of that theme." The chord accompanying each figure contains the same number of notes as the figure itself, and these chords are, of course, derived from the row. The form of the row used melodically in the first period of the theme turns up in the harmonic accompaniment of the last, and vice versa; the second and third periods exchange horizontal and vertical elements in like manner.

The coming of the row dealt the death blow to the tonal universe. The concept of order changed sides, so to speak, for while post-tonal music was doomed to anarchy, living music held at last the key to a dialectical organization, which was ultimately to engender a new form of poetics. In order for these objectives to be fully realized, however, it was still necessary to do away with the two last mainstays of tonal music: theme and the continuity of musical discourse. An approach to music capable of revolutionizing sensibility and of fostering the rigorous elaboration of free forms had necessarily to be *discontinuous* and *athematic*. This was to be the eventual justification for the incredible, unprecedented leap which music had just taken. But in 1923 these truths were still completely hidden. One might imagine that Schönberg set out to discover them. It hardly seems possible that such a fine mind as his should have failed to see the unlimited field of exploration that lay before him. And yet, the preceding analysis of the Variations, op. 31 shows that its composer was concerned with entirely different problems. The rules governing the row phenomenon had hardly been laid down when they slipped beyond the grasp of their originator.

Schönberg's Decline

Schönberg reached the zenith of his career with the invention of the twelve-tone row. He devoted his "third period" (1923–1930) to the application of his discovery, but the works produced were a far cry, aesthetically, from the best of his previous music. Here and there, of course, they do contain some lovely passages. But the acute polyphonic struggle which lends interest to the exposition of the Suite (Septet), op. 29, or the remarkable poetic qualities of the third variation in the third movement of this same work, do not make up for its extreme dryness as a whole. It would seem that, in Schönberg's case, the invention of a new language was accompanied by a loss of sensibility. To put it more accurately, his sensibility was unable to adapt itself to the new musical conceptions. A basic antagonism separated the hyper-romantic composer of *Erwartung* from the technique born of his creative intellect, and this discrepancy grew steadily with the passing years. A form of academicism wormed its way into the works of this once daring artist, preparing the way for his "fourth period," which coincided with his removal to the United States. The California climate seemed to inspire him as little as it did his great rival, Stravinsky. The similarity of their careers continued even then, for these two incomparable artists, who had done such brilliant work in the years around 1910, slowly burnt themselves out through middle and old age, writing all but insignificant music, in which they seemed, at times, to repudiate their previous accomplishments.

Schönberg's greatness consisted in the discovery of a new language; his failing—as we shall see—lay in his inability to realize that this language implied an *exhaustive* reappraisal of form in music. For the works that Schönberg went on to forge with his new-found tool took the form of suites, sonatas, themes and variations, rondos, and the like. He obviously looked upon the row, not as a new thought-form, but merely as a handy device. Schönberg had broken new paths but had no clear notion of where they led. This is why, despite their occasional merits, his "third period" works were comparatively so weak. Actually, it was perfectly natural that this exceptional creator should have displayed such limitations. One can never break completely with one's background, and Schönberg belonged to a generation which was infatuated with classical rhetoric and for which a convulsive form of expressionism was the essence of art. Schönberg's attitude during his years of silence attests to the fact that his rigorous mind was well aware of the destructive role he had played in undermining the tonal structure and was left unsatisfied by the paroxysmic expressionism of *Erwartung* and the Five Pieces, op. 16. We now know that Schönberg had always intended to use the row, not as a means of transcending the tonal order, but of rebuilding it on new foundations. Most of his late works were to be devoted to this task, which the organic requirements of his art had led him to abandon for a time, leaving his disciple, Alban Berg, to carry it on alone. Similarly, he became absorbed by the problem of filling in the last gaps in the tonal order. "The harmony in my Organ Variations," he writes, "bridges the gap between my chamber music and dissonant music." Schönberg's outlook in his old age was plainly backward-looking and out of step with history. The *Ode to Napoleon*, to name only the best of his fourth-period works, was written in a so-called twelve-tone tonality; this attempt to create a new form of tonality based on the tone-row is, in the last analysis, utterly meaningless.[1]

Schönberg's influence, which is now considerable, has been felt on several levels. One of his chief contributions was the rehabilitating of "serious" music, partially discredited by the plethora of "light" music resulting from the misconstrued examples of Ravel and Stravinsky. Though the keynote of the Viennese master's career was a relentless pursuit of "expressiveness" in music, he came to grant an increasing importance to musical ideas *per se*. He never made the slightest concession to recreational music (the chance echo of a Viennese waltz notwithstanding); this would have been completely incompatible with his austere ideals. The best elements of today's younger generation, impatient with the frivolity of their immediate elders, have been greatly attracted by this attitude, and it has done much for the expansion of twelve-tone music.

Arnold Schönberg was one of the most efficiently destructive forces in the history of Western art. Oddly enough, his most

---

[1] Mr. Leibowitz is undoubtedly right in pointing out that the tonality here is extremely "loose," owing to constant modulations and a hyper-chromatic style of writing, but it constitutes a throwback nevertheless. The doubling of certain instruments at the octave may be regarded as another concession to the past.

passionate desire was to be constructive, but by an unfortunate twist of fate, Schönberg, who remained an exceptional creator so long as he was busy destroying, ceased to be truly creative as soon as he tried to construct. Like Moses, he may have shown the way to the Promised Land, but was never allowed to enter it himself.

CHAPTER THREE

Alban Berg

Berg's Career

Alban Berg was born in Vienna on February 9, 1885. Though they gave him no particular encouragement, his middle-class parents did not stand in the way of their son's musical vocation. While pursuing his secondary studies, he was thus able to devote much of his free time to the composition of *lieder*. His choice of a career was finally determined by his elder brother; he secretly showed some of Alban's songs to Schönberg, who agreed to accept the young man as his pupil. Thus in 1904 began a friendship which was to last far longer than the six years during which Berg studied with the older man.

If we disregard the many *lieder* written during that period— as well as a Theme and Variations for piano, still unpublished —the catalogue of Berg's works begins with the Piano Sonata, op. 1 (1907–1908). This was followed by Four Songs, op. 2 and the First Quartet, op. 3 (1910), composed under the watchful eye of Schönberg. In 1911 Berg married, and in order to earn a living was forced to do transcriptions. In 1913, Schönberg first presented Berg's music to the public, by including his *Picture Postcard* Songs, op. 4 (1911–1912), in a program of chamber music; the ensuing outcry had its aftermath in court. The Three Orchestral Pieces, op. 6, begun shortly before the outbreak of hostilities, was finished at the end of 1914. A few months later, Berg was mobilized. He had, however, suffered from asthma since adolescence, and his frequent attacks released him from active duty. He was assigned to the War Ministry, and it was there that he put the finishing touches on the libretto of *Wozzeck*, the great work of his career.

In May, 1914, Berg attended a performance of the Büchner play and immediately decided to do an opera based upon it. He revised the original text, retaining only fifteen of Büchner's twenty-six scenes. The score was begun in 1917 and completed in 1921. Hermann Scherchen conducted a fragmentary performance of the work in Frankfurt on June 11, 1924. At Erich Kleiber's instigation, the Berlin Opera staged it the following year; the first performance was given on December 14, 1925, and *Wozzeck* remained part of the Berlin repertory until Hitler came to power. An extensive tour in 1929 brought it to the attention of audiences in the German provinces and in several foreign cities (Amsterdam, Zurich, Philadelphia, New York, and London).

Berg's fame—actually a relative fame, as he was practically unknown in the Latin countries—had only a temporary effect on his standard of living, and during the last years of his life he was often sorely pressed. He wrote less and less music as the years went by: the Chamber Concerto (1923–1925), the Lyric Suite for string quartet (1925–1926), and the cantata *Der Wein* (1929). His last work was the Violin Concerto, commissioned by Louis Krasner, but dedicated "to the memory of an angel"

(*Dem Andenken eines Engels*); the "angel" was Manon Gropius—the daughter of the famous architect and Alma Maria Mahler—who died at the age of eighteen. Berg composed this score in an unusually short time (from April to August, 1935), as though he sensed that it was to have the same ominous significance as Mozart's *Requiem*. In order to complete it, he stopped orchestrating his second opera, *Lulu*, which, as it turned out, was never completed, but which he had worked on from 1928 until 1934. Berg never heard either of these works; he contracted blood-poisoning from a neglected abscess and died on December 24, 1935.

Alban Berg was a perfect example of the post-romantic Austrian artist, haunted by the anguish of one of history's most somber periods. The few existing photographs reveal a face ravaged by inward suffering. At eighteen he tried to commit suicide. His propensity for dramatic expression, which he carried to almost delirious extremes (as an adolescent he wrote letters in the style of Peter Altenberg's poetry) made him one of the leading figures in the German expressionist movement.

The Instrumental Works

Berg's development bears remarkable similarities to that of Schönberg. Both went through the same four "periods," and in the same chronological order: tonal and then non-tonal post-romanticism, non-tonal row composition, and finally the return to a "new" tonality based on the row. Berg's career, however, was not as evenly divided among these four periods as was Schönberg's. For example, Schönberg's early tonal post-romanticism occupied only a very brief span in his disciple's career; the teacher's experience in this field partly spared the pupil from having to go through it again. Aesthetically, however, Berg was branded for life by the post-romantic music which so absorbed him in his youth and which was, moreover, deeply in tune with his character. At first, Berg was very strongly influenced by Schönberg, following in his footsteps, adopting his discoveries one after the other; but he stole a march on his teacher toward the end of his life when he "revived" tonality through the tone-row technique. (This was originally Schönberg's idea, but as we have seen, he was unable to put it into practice until late in life.)

Berg's music, though essentially expressionistic and dramatic, is nonetheless sustained by an acute sense of form; this is one of the many qualities generally—and quite rightly—admired in his chamber music. As early as his Sonata, op. 1, he displayed a deep concern for the structural problems facing composers of his generation. This Sonata is obviously influenced by Schönberg's Chamber Symphony, and like it, grows entirely from a single idea exposed in the first measures. The work already makes use of the cyclical approach which Berg developed more fully in the large works of his maturity; every theme and every important development is "telegraphed," as it were, before it actually appears, and is invariably referred to afterward in the course of the work.

The Sonata and the Songs, op. 2, with their heavy, Wagnerian flavor, are Berg's only tonal music, in the conventional sense of the term. Already, the Quartet, op. 3, was a step beyond the bounds of tonality, based as it was on a functional use of the interval. The half tone, in particular, determined most of the work's pivotal figures. But though at that time Berg did have a tendency to do away with themes, he seemed neither to feel a basic need to do so, nor to realize the structural implications of this step. The Pieces for Clarinet and Piano—his sole attempt at the "small form"—displayed a great economy of means but remained, as Michel Fano puts it, "photographic reductions" of the conventional structures to which they still clung. Though not actually a slave to traditional forms, Berg, like Schönberg, never quite managed to break away from them.

Ten years later, at the height of his maturity, Berg returned to chamber music with the Chamber Concerto and the Lyric Suite. In the words of Michel Fano, from whom I have borrowed a description of this work, the Chamber Concerto displays

> the most extraordinary degree of formal rigor that he [Berg] ever attained. Its deeply theatrical nature is, however, revealed, by the work's "expressive" aspect, and by its use of certain special effects, . . . such as the musical dedication—based on the names of Schönberg, Webern, and Berg—which occurs at the beginning of the work and constitutes its formative cell, the "dramatic" personification of the solo instruments, and the application of the *parlando* technique to the violin. . . . The instrumental makeup of the concerto varies with each of its three movements. The first is scored for piano and winds, the second for violin and winds, and the third for piano, violin, and winds. . . . The first movement—prefaced by the dedication—is a theme and variations; it constituted the first large-scale application of the inverted, retrograde, and retrograde-inverted forms. In the second movement, the recapitulation is the strict retrograde of the exposition. This was a large-scale application of a technique used by Webern on a "molecular" scale. In the final movement, which is preceded by a cadenza for the two solo instruments, the components of the two other movements are superposed and finally eliminated one by one. The Concerto constituted the next-to-the-last stage on the way to an absolute mastery of the twelve-tone technique—finally attained by Webern; it proves, however, that Berg could not really master the system without overcoming the dramatist in him, for that side of his nature was incompatible with the true spirit of row music.

The Lyric Suite for string quartet, generally considered Berg's finest instrumental work, displays the same basically dramatic character. This score was a frank attempt to convey paroxysmic emotions, or so we are led to believe by the titles of its movements: 1. *Allegro giovale;* 2. *Andante amoroso;* 3. *Allegro misterioso* (containing a *Trio estatico*); 4. *Adagio appassionato;* 5. *Presto delirando* (containing a middle section marked *Tenebroso*); 6. *Largo desolato*. And yet, here again, the sentiments depicted go hand in hand with a brilliantly articulated cyclical construction, the perfect balance of which strengthens the overall sense of unity.

From a technical point of view, the Lyric Suite is composed alternately of passages written according to the row system and passages which are not. It is possible that Berg handled the row with greater subtlety than that displayed by Schönberg during those same years (1925 and 1926). The *Allegro misterioso* movement is particularly interesting in this respect; in it Berg applied two new concepts: *permutation* and *derivative rows*.

FIG. 4

The first four notes of the original row—B-flat, A, F, B—form a *sub-group* in this movement which, through the permutation of its component notes takes on four distinct shapes, each of which recurs in identical form in one of the transpositions of the row (Fig. 4). Berg made clever use of the ambiguities arising from this situation but, like his teacher, he was too deeply imbued with conventional notions to realize the far-reaching implications of these ambiguities. Once they began to treat the row as a theme, it was not surprising that both he and Schönberg should end by trying to reconsider tonality in terms of the row.

This project may be considered Berg's last will and testament, for he did not carry it out completely until his very last work, the Violin Concerto. The twelve-note row on which this work is built comprises, first of all, two minor chords and two major chords disposed at intervals of a fifth—and stated on the open strings of the violin—followed by the first four notes of a whole-tone scale (a reference to the initial phrase of the Bach chorale, *Es ist Genug*). This formative row (Fig. 5) contains all the basic elements of the tonal and structural developments of the entire concerto: on the one hand a tonic-dominant relationship, and on the other a choral theme which predominates

FIG. 5

throughout the final peroration (probably the source of a similar device in Honegger's String Symphony which, like Berg's Concerto, is written in a "loose" tonality). Though the work is highly ingenious and well put together, one is surprised to find a revival of the notion of alternating consonance and dissonance, and consequently the ebb and flow of tension which had sustained Western music for so many centuries. One cannot help wondering what purpose the row serves in this conception.

The Operas

Berg's best music, however, is to be found, of course, in his operas. It was only natural that a composer who allowed his brilliant dramatic flair to creep into the most austere forms of chamber music should feel most at home in opera. His predilection for this medium became clear as early as 1912, in the *Picture Postcard* song cycle with orchestral accompaniment, which, insofar as this is a set form at all, went far beyond its conventional limits. These pieces foreshadowed *Wozzeck* and *Lulu* in several ways; besides bearing certain thematic relationships to the operas, they also employ similarly lavish—not to say extravagant—vocal and orchestral devices and derived from an architectural-aesthetic concept involving the incorporation of large instrumental forms (in the case of the *Postcard* cycle, a passacaglia) into a dramatic structure.

Wozzeck is Berg's masterpiece. The composer of the *Picture Postcard* cycle could not fail to be attracted by Büchner's drama and its rather special brand of romanticism. The play's astonishingly modern theme does not deal with gods, feudal lords, knights in armor, or other legendary heroes, but with a poor fellow driven to crime and near-madness by the malicious stupidity of those around him and by his own wretched lot. Berg extracted a maximum of dramatic intensity from this situation. The work's highly complex musical structure forms an integral part of the plot. The fusion of music and drama achieved in *Wozzeck* attests to Berg's extraordinary intellectual powers, for he had the audacity to fit each scene into the framework of a large symphonic form. This was no ear-catching stunt; on the contrary, as Berg himself said, "no one in the audience should ever be aware of these fugues, inventions, suites, sonata fragments, variations, and passacaglias." This statement is often misinterpreted; Berg did not mean that emotions are more important than form, but that the two are indivisible.

Each of the five scenes which compose Act One serves to introduce a new character (Wozzeck himself remaining constantly in the foreground, whether or not he is actually on stage) and is in the form of a clearly defined set-piece: 1. Suite; 2. Rhapsody; 3. Military March and Lullaby; 4. Passacaglia; 5. Andante. The five scenes of Act Two follow the dramatic development quite closely and form a kind of symphony in five movements: 1. Allegro in sonata form; 2. Fantasy and Fugue; 3. Largo; 4. Scherzo; 5. Introduction and Rondo. The six scenes of the final and climactic Act Three are handled as a set of inventions on 1. a theme; 2. a note; 3. a rhythm; 4. a six-note chord; 5. a tonality; 6. a perpetual motion. The opera has no overture, but the various scenes are punctuated by symphonic interludes.

The powerful dramatic functions assigned to certain intervals and even to certain notes, the wide expressive range of Berg's orchestration (which nevertheless avoids all the pitfalls of post-Wagnerian bombast) and his use of "rhythmic declamation" derived from the *Sprechgesang* of *Pierrot Lunaire*, all contribute to make *Wozzeck* the most characteristically modern of operas. It is, of course, open to criticism on several counts. For one thing, Berg restored the Wagnerian leitmotif which Schönberg had been able to dispense with in *Erwartung*, and although the intrusion of a D-minor interlude in an otherwise non-tonal context may be dramatically effective, it is in rather bad taste from a purely musical standpoint (the redundancy of this section is enough to condemn it, in any case). Nevertheless, the score is full of splendid sections, and the interest is sustained throughout. Some of the most famous passages are: the breathtaking three-part fugue in Act Two which conveys an astonishing portrayal of madness; the famous crescendo on the note B— probably the most extraordinary dramatic effect ever devised —which promptly gives way to the strains of a pianola in a striking effect of contrast; Wozzeck's drowning scene, suggested rather than depicted by the orchestra, and the very last page of the work, which constitutes the high point of a symbolic language that underlies the entire opera. (This symbolism in musical discourse is perhaps the most archaic aspect of Berg's art, but his genius enabled him to shift it onto a structural level, thereby creating a world of memories and premonitions which, over and above its purely theatrical implications, may well have foreshadowed the dream-like universe of Jean Barraqué; in this sense his symbolism is the most modern side of Berg's music.)

In composing *Lulu*, Berg was rarely as successful as he had been with his first opera. The work is uneven and occasionally quite lurid (especially in the first tableaux). Seldom does it attain the level of dramatic excitement which made *Wozzeck* so admirable. *Lulu* also reveals a basic contradiction between theatrical imperatives and the tone-row technique. One might even say that in the context of the expressionist opera as Berg conceived it, the row was rather superfluous.

To my mind, any objective study of Berg's music leads inevitably to this conclusion. With the exception of a few isolated pages—such as the *Allegro misterioso* in the Lyric Suite—Berg merely used the row system without grasping its real implications. The row is not essential to the spirit of his music; on the contrary, there are times when it is actually a hindrance. Berg had a fine sense of structure and his sensibility was most at ease within the self-imposed formal structures of *Wozzeck*. This is the work which will ensure Berg's lasting fame as a composer; it stands out as the only major opera written since *Pelleas*, and its composer as the greatest dramatic genius of our time, probably our only composer to be compared with Monteverdi or Moussorgsky. Berg, although a full-fledged disciple of Schönberg, outstripped his teacher in this particular field and founded a school of his own; one cannot say as much for any other Schönberg disciple, not even Křenek. Berg already has disciples in his own right; Hans Werner Henze and, to a lesser extent, Menotti, are both influenced by Berg's concepts.

Twenty-five years have passed since Berg's death and he has not yet become a "popular" composer. His admirers, on the other hand, often rank him very high. Some, neglecting the accusation of "morbidity" so often levelled against works like *Wozzeck*, or the Three Orchestral Pieces, op. 6, look upon them as the high-points of an ultra-romantic music which was merely portended in Schönberg's *Erwartung* and Five Pieces, op. 16. As with Schönberg and Stravinsky, the last stage of Berg's musical career is undoubtedly open to criticism; his case, however, is different. Berg, less destructive than Schönberg and less original than Stravinsky, appears to me as the last representative of a great tradition. It is a pity that he wasted the last years of his life in a sterile attempt to retrace his steps, recapitulating the attainments of his predecessors. But then Berg may simply not have been equipped to venture onto the deserted shores of a new world.

CHAPTER FOUR

Anton Webern

Biography and Catalogue of Works

In contrast with Stravinsky's glittering biography, which reads like the ideal success story, Webern's career offers little anecdotal material for the biographer. Though of noble lineage, Anton von Webern seems to have dropped the particle from his name at an early age, for it appears on none of the published scores to which I have had access. Born in Vienna on December 3, 1883, he began his career as a musicologist, and did work on Heinrich Isaac. In 1902 he studied counterpoint with Guido Adler. It was not until 1904, however, that he and his friend Alban Berg met Schönberg, who steered him onto the path of composition. For Webern, however, this path never led to fame or even notoriety; indeed, though his music was supremely revolutionary, it never created more than one or two minor scandals. He conducted theater orchestras in Austria and Germany, conducted on the Vienna radio, and was the principal conductor of the Vienna Workers' Symphony Concerts from 1922 until 1934. After the Nazi *putsch*, Webern was obliged to take the menial job of proofreader for one of Vienna's largest music publishers.

As it happens, this obscure existence was in keeping with the man's great modesty and apparent lack of ambition. Ironically enough, the one unusual feature of his career was his death, which occurred under rather mysterious circumstances: this harmless, gentle man, whose only passions in life were music and flowers, was accidentally shot down in his Mittersill garden by an American MP on September 15, 1945. At the time, however, his death caused very little stir. It is Pierre Boulez who deserves credit for having revealed the true significance of Webern's music.

The catalogue of Webern's works is even smaller than Berg's; it contains more titles, of course, but nothing Webern wrote is nearly as long as *Wozzeck* or *Lulu*. It consists of a Passacaglia for orchestra, op. 1, *Enflieht auf leichten Kähnen* for *a cappella* chorus, op. 2 (1908), the Songs op. 3 and 4, Five Movements for string quartet, op. 5 (1909), Six Pieces for orchestra, op. 6, Four Pieces for violin and piano, op. 7 (1910), Two Songs, op. 8, (1911–1912), Six Bagatelles for string quartet, op. 9, Five Pieces for orchestra, op. 10 (1913), Three Pieces for 'cello and piano, op. 11 (1914), the Songs, op. 12 (1915–1917), 13 (1916), 14 (1917–1921), and 15 (1923), Five Canons for voice, clarinet, and bass clarinet, op. 16, the Songs, op. 17 (1924)—in these songs he used the tone-row technique for the first time—the Songs with clarinet and guitar, op. 18 (1925), the Songs for mixed chorus, op. 19 (1926), the String Trio, op. 20 (1927), the Symphony, op. 21 (1928), the Quartet for violin, clarinet, saxophone, and piano, op. 22 (1930), Three Songs, op. 23, the Concerto for Nine Instruments, op. 24 (1934), Three Songs, op. 25 (1934), *Das Augenlicht* for mixed chorus and orchestra, op. 26

(1935), the Piano Variations, op. 27 (1936), the String Quartet, op. 28 (1938), two Cantatas, op. 29 (1939) and 31 (1941–1943), the Variations for orchestra, op. 30 (1940) and a number of orchestral transcriptions, one of which, at least—that of the six-part *ricercar* from the *Musical Offering*—may be regarded as an original work.

Webern's "Aural Sensibility"

Because Berg and Webern were Schönberg's favorite pupils there is a widespread tendency to assign them identical roles in the world-famous trinity of the Vienna school. This gives one, however, a false perspective, for while it is true that the composer of *Wozzeck* was Schönberg's spiritual son, Webern's debt to his teacher was limited to his early training and a few key ideas which helped him to clarify his own thinking. The example of Berg and Webern, who not only belonged to the same generation and moved in the same circles but were bound together by a lasting friendship, and yet whose individual temperaments and conceptions were irrevocably opposed, is probably unique in the history of Western music.

As Pierre Boulez puts it: "Schönberg and Berg both belong to the twilight years of the great German romantic tradition, which they brought to its peak in such luxuriant, flamboyant works as *Pierrot Lunaire* and *Wozzeck;* whereas Webern—steering a course that led, as it were, through Debussy—reacted strongly against all forms of inherited rhetoric in his effort to rehabilitate the power of sheer sound." This reference to Debussy should come as a surprise to no one, save those narrow technicians so involved with the structural problems raised by Webern's music that they fail to grasp its essence. Webern's renovation of musical language cannot be explained without referring to a form of sensibility that both preceded and justified it. The fact that Schönberg, despite his amazing inventions, already seems a composer of the past, and not such a recent past at that, is probably due precisely to his shallow understanding of Debussy's message.

In the prelude to his *Martyre de Saint Sébastien*, Debussy made use of a series of parallel aggregations which cannot be interpreted as *chords*, but rather as *note-groups*, designed to "embellish" the melodic line. Webern appropriated this concept and developed, within the framework of the row technique, a *complex of notes* which is neither a chord (it involves no precise harmonic functions) nor the accompaniment to a melody (Webern gradually eliminated melody from his music, in any case). Thus, if we consider them separately, the complexes of notes in the Cantata, op. 31, foreshadow the *"objets sonores"* used in the so-called *musique concrète*. Jean Barraqué has clearly emphasized the affiliation between Debussy's and Webern's aural sensibilities, demonstrating how the Austrian, in his greater concern for organization, made more extensive application of the Frenchman's intuitive discoveries. Barraqué writes:

> Debussy, in his most interesting orchestrations, at least, broke up the melody and scattered brief motifs throughout the different levels of the orchestra, creating, so to speak, a scale of tone-colors. The structures of his later works—and especially *Jeux*—are based upon the superposition and juxtaposition of independent patterns which he subjected, both in their rhythmic texture and melodic outline, to a very free process of variation. Debussy split up the orchestra into single cells and used polyphony to outline them. Profiting by this achievement, as well as by his own experience with polyphony, Webern thus found himself able to deal with an entirely new musical material: tone-color *per se*. Debussy had revolutionized the traditional orchestral concepts of harmonic pedal-point, instrumental groups, and so forth; Webern replaced the notion of instrumental groups with the less conventional one of tone-color groups. But, above all, he allotted the orchestra a *functional* role. Since the order of

intervals was now rationally determined by the tone-row, a more consistent treatment of the orchestra was possible, through the use of techniques such as the canon (e.g., the first movement of the Symphony—in which subject and counter-subject are linked together in the form of tiny, shifting cells—or the Quartet, op. 22). This conception of musical phenomena endowed the word *polyphony* with a broader and deeper meaning; the musical components were dissociated and reorganized in such a way as to tighten the bonds between them, establishing their equality with respect to one another as well as the indivisibility of the whole.

At the same time, Webern borrowed from Schönberg the notion of *Klangfarbenmelodie*. His extremely keen ear enabled him to handle the tone-color of each instrument with great precision, whence the very special coloring of his orchestral works. He also uses the *Klangfarbenmelodie* to conceal structures which might otherwise seem too obvious. In the double canon at the beginning of the Symphony, op. 21, each of the four parts shifts successively from one instrument to another, ranging from French horn to clarinet and from harp to 'cello.

Whereas almost none of Schönberg's row music ever equalled *Pierrot Lunaire* for sheer beauty of sound, Webern seems to have been far better equipped for this type of writing; in *Das Augenlicht* he devised a vocal polyphony which, despite a certain rigidity due to the alternating of homophonic and contrapuntal passages, attained a very high degree of aural refinement. The overly linear character of this work, its lack of rhythmic fluidity, and the rather fragmentary nature of its *Klangfarbenmelodie*, a technique which Webern had not yet completely mastered in 1935, may seem rather "outdated" now; on the other hand, the perfect aural balance achieved in this work attests to Webern's "pre-auditive" mastery of twelve-tone writing (Fig. 6), the like of which it would be difficult to find in any other work written prior to World War II. High-

FIG. 6*

* Anton Webern, *Das Augenlicht.* Copyright © 1956 by Universal Edition A. G., Vienna. Reprinted by permission of the above and their English and American agents: Universal Edition (London) Ltd. and Associated Music Publishers, Inc., New York.

lighted by incisive instrumental contours, this smooth choral block has a splendid resonance.

Organization and Dialectics

Webern was the first composer since Debussy to have been in love with sound for its own sake, and this fact was to condition his whole style of composition. With even more vehemence than Debussy, he too adopted Verlaine's precept and "wrung the neck of eloquence." Spurning all the large, established forms, he set out to explore the new musical world in a small number of highly condensed works, gradually evolving a concept described by Jean Barraqué as *musical dialectics*. Schönberg undoubtedly deserves a good deal of credit for this development; it was he, after all, who first laid down the rules of row composition. But though Webern was less minutely systematic than his teacher, the new technique was in close harmony with his own personal conceptions for he had, in fact, composed scores prior to Schönberg's invention which were already in the spirit of row music. His Five Movements for string quartet prove that as early as 1909 Webern had conceived of a "spatial organization of sound"—the phrase is Michel Fano's—which is the very essence of row music. It is therefore not surprising that, alongside Schönberg's large-scale works, in which the row was used to restore conventional thematic notions and the traditional oscillation between harmonic and contrapuntal writing, a more revolutionary attitude should appear which challenged the time-worn concepts of theme and accompanied melodic line. Webern was destined in every way to be the originator of this purified conception of row composition: by his disdain for "big music," by his craving for rigor, and by his sensibility which, unlike that of his peers, was not hampered by vestiges of romanticism.

Webern was the apostle of "the small form." Most of his music consists of incredibly short pieces, some of which take less than a minute to perform. Why this exaggerated conciseness? Because the elaboration of a new language was an extremely difficult task for Webern—we may infer this from the small number of his works—and only by tackling them one at a time could he solve the problems that faced him. Moreover, his obsession with formal perfection deterred him from attacking overly complex material; he preferred deliberately to limit himself. The best-known example of this attitude is the row on which his Quartet, op. 28, is built (Fig. 7); it is divided into three identical cells, of which the second is the inversion of the first and the third a transposition of the first, thus greatly narrowing the range of possibilities open to the composer. The brevity of Webern's works is the price he had to pay for their density. The fact remains that, on the formal level, each of his works constitutes an intensive treatment of a specific problem posed in its most basic terms.

Webern's music reaches the listener's ear as a pattern of geometrical figures in sound, symmetrical at times, asymmetrical at others or, more precisely, asymmetrical within a symmetrical framework. The melodic development customary in tonal

FIG. 7

music is replaced by an organized succession of rhythmic and melodic combinations, clearly differentiated in time. The first measures of the Variations for Piano, for example, contain the statement of two parallel rows, one in each hand (Fig. 8); when these reach the halfway point, i.e. the second beat in the fourth measure, the right-hand row is taken up in the left hand and vice versa. Now, since these two rows are actually two aspects of the same row (one is the retrograde of the other) the notes that lie on either side of that second beat are mirror images of each other (though the second does contain an interesting

rhythmic variant). The subsequent sections, each of which
offers a different aspect of the same row combined with new
rhythmic and melodic patterns, are built on this same principle
of the mirror canon or *Spiegelbild* which was, along with the
ordinary canon, Webern's favorite structure.

FIG. 8*

Thus, Webern was gradually moving toward a music in
which the notions of theme and development would no longer
be meaningful. Of course, the awareness that this was a *necessary* development came to him quite slowly. He often resorted
to classical structures, and especially to the sonata form (as in
the opening movements of opp. 22 and 27). But while Schönberg had only glimpsed the possibility of an "athematic" music
Webern was the first to have a clear notion of it. This composer
who, in his opus 23, devised one of the loveliest of all non-tonal
melodies, was also the first to challenge the sacrosanctity of
melodic line.

I need hardly emphasize the fact that Webern's music, especially in his later works, was subject to an unbending discipline. Not only did he organize the melodic structures and figures determined by the notes and their order, but he extended
this organization to include components which tonal composers had never handled so precisely, and which were to play

* Anton Webern, Variations for Piano. Copyright 1937 by Universal Edition A.
G., Vienna. Reprinted by permission of the above and their English and American
agents: Universal Edition (London) Ltd. and Associated Music Publishers, Inc.,
New York.

an important role in serial composition. Tone-colors, registers, attacks, intensities, and even silence itself—in short all those elements which had hitherto provided only a vague, expressionist coloring—were incorporated by Webern into a truly cosmic organization of the musical material.

As a logical extension of the concept of absolute-variation inherited from Schönberg, Webern went on to include orchestral tone-color among the materials subject to variation. On the other hand, it was a desire for greater textural refinement that led him to organize instrumental registers. He was also the first to have proscribed the use of the octave, a principle which all major twelve-tone composers now consider as basic to their art as was the ban on consecutive octaves and fifths to that of classical composers. Lastly, few composers have had Webern's intuitive understanding of that negative component of music, silence, which he eventually incorporated into his dialectic. As Pierre Boulez has remarked, "this was Webern's sole rhythmic discovery, but it was of shattering significance."

Webern: Pioneer of a New Musical Order

Just what was Webern's contribution to music? Though he did not invent the row system himself, he was the first composer who actually needed it as a catalyst for his creative powers. Though he inherited the structural technique known as *Spiegelbild* from Schönberg (who had gotten it from the old contrapuntilists), it was Webern who first incorporated it into a brand-new conception of polyphony. Similarily, his methods of organizing tone-color and registers gave specific content to another of Schönberg's ideas, the *Klangfarbenmelodie*. Schönberg also bequeathed to him a fondness for extremely wide intervals; Webern carried the principle so far as to dismember the melodic line completely—in defiance, at times, of the actual capacities of the human voice (this tendency can be traced back to Debussy).

The beauty of Webern's musical universe, its very dimensions, in fact, cannot but elude the grasp of music-lovers bred exclusively on the classical tradition. The underlying sensibility which infuses life into his music is, perhaps, its most hidden facet; in the words of Pierre Boulez, "his sensibility is so strikingly new that it may seem to demand a purely intellectual approach." Oddly enough, some of his contemporaries ironically dubbed Webern "the composer with the *pianissimo expressivo*." Though this joke misses its mark completely, it does help to explain why performers often have such a mistaken approach to his works. Certain performances conducted by Hermann Scherchen have shown that a correct interpretation of Webern requires absolute rigor and an utter contempt for "expressive" lights and shades. Webern was the forerunner of an "abstract music" which was later to be developed by Boulez, Stockhausen, and a few others. He was the first to reject every kind of sentimental appurtenance, distilling beauty into form alone. Webern's music, like the best of Stravinsky's, constitutes a courageous break with the past. And despite the great differences between them, the belated tribute paid to Webern by the aging composer of *The Rite of Spring* is very significant, insofar as the celebrated artist recognizes the humble proofreader as his spiritual brother.

Webern's music, I feel, confirms the postulate set forth in my introductory chapter. There is no reason why this musical Columbus should be expected to have written works comparable to those of Bach or Beethoven. His music is like Mallarmé's poetry in that its influence is probably greater than its intrinsic worth; it is limited by its own asceticism and, despite its technical perfection, by the impression of incompleteness it inevitably produces. Webern's greatness lay in the extreme rigor of his creative effort and in that hermit-like courage which enabled him to feel that the arid "laboratory stage" of music was not beneath him. These were the qualities that equipped him to become the very first explorer of an uncharted world. As Webern slowly groped his way toward a hitherto undreamt-of horizon, he would occasionally stop and retrace his steps; it was as though, standing on the threshold of the unknown, he had felt a sudden dizzy spell. It is hard to find any other explanation for the weak spots in his late works; the finale of his very last score, in particular, the Cantata, op. 31, is based on stilted, almost academic repetitions of canonic figures, reminiscent of the worst neoclassicism. Webern, like his great contemporaries, succumbed to the curse which seems to have plagued them all toward the ends of their lives.

For a long time his music had no repercussions at all, but its influence has grown steadily since his death. An increasing number of young composers are gathering behind his banner. It seems doubtful, however, that Webern will ever become a favorite with the general public, or that his Symphony will ever be as popular as the Unfinished or the *Fantastique*. This lack of popularity may seem unjust, but it is perfectly understandable, and in choosing to follow the path he did, Webern implicitly accepted this fate.

The musical conceptions of Webern and his followers, which consist in an attempt to communicate sensibility by means of a dialectic, are criticized by opponents of "abstraction" in art for their cosmic and, in one sense, inhuman aspect. But in another sense, these conceptions are by no means inhuman, for the artificial can be more truly "human" than the "natural," in the original connotation of these words. Besides, it seems to me rather presumptuous to settle mankind's future so soon. Can any of us possibly know what our descendants will be like, or how closely they will actually resemble us? On the other hand, the music being written today can, perhaps, provide a key to the world of tomorrow—on the sole condition, however, that we are capable of deciphering it correctly, for the meaning of an artist's message is sometimes cloudier than that of its historical context. Let us therefore confine ourselves to a close scrutiny of the music of our time.

Contemporary composers who do not adhere to the row system derive their incentive to create from an ardent search for a form of expression that may counteract the great movement whose early stages we have just studied. This is exactly what Chopin was doing only a few years after the death of Beethoven, for the latter's contributions to music would seem to have left no room for the former's aesthetic conceptions, derived as they were from such totally different values. Therefore, though Webern remains the greatest composer of his generation, it is only fitting that his chapter be followed by one devoted to another great composer who developed his music outside the row system: Béla Bartók.

Was Bartók's music "Hungarian first and foremost," as many of his fervent admirers maintain, or was it the fruit of a common heritage which encompasses the music of France, Russia, and every other European country? The problem is of small concern to me and I shall not argue it here. I am more interested in defining the essential features of a musical conception which is not far removed from neoclassicism, in some respects, but which has other, more absorbing aspects. At his best, I feel that Bartók may have managed to blend a modern attitude toward musical poetics with an idiom which was just conventional enough to give a large audience immediate access to his music. This may be why his music, often so pleasing to the ear, is so popular at present, but it is also why one may have doubts as to its immortality.

CHAPTER FIVE

Béla Bartók

Bartók's Career; Bartók the Man

Béla Bartók was born in Nagy-Szentmiklós, Hungary, on March 25, 1881. His wealthy, middle-class parents steered him toward music at an early age. He entered the Budapest Royal Academy where he studied composition with Hans Koessler and piano with Itsván Thomán, to whose teaching post he succeeded in 1907. While still in their teens, he and his friends Ernst Dohnányi and Zoltan Kodály took a fiercely patriotic stand in favor of Hungarian independence. Bartók even went so far as to poke fun at the Austrian national anthem in his symphonic poem *Kossuth* (1903). Among his other early works are Burlesque (1904), two Suites (1905–1907), *Deux Portraits* (1907–1908), and *Deux Images* (1910), all for orchestra, a Piano Quintet (1905), and the First String Quartet (1907), plus a number of piano scores: the Bagatelles (1908),

Elegies and Children's Suite (1908–1909), Four Dirges (1910), and the *Allegro Barbaro* (1911).

In 1911 an official jury, appointed to select the "best Hungarian opera," rejected *Duke Bluebeard's Castle*, written by Bartók and Béla Balasz. This work—Bartók's only opera—was staged successfully by the Budapest Opera seven years later. Balasz also provided the book for Bartók's ballet *The Wooden Prince*, which, like the Second String Quartet, was composed during the first World War. These works were followed by the *Études* for piano (1918), the ballet *The Miraculous Mandarin* (1919), two sonatas for violin and piano (1921–1922), and the Dance Suite for orchestra (1923), which was Bartók's first big international success. During this same period, Bartók began an intermittent and somewhat checkered career as a concert pianist, which took him to most of the larger cities of Europe and the United States.

In 1923 the composer lapsed into a period of silence which did not end until 1926 with the Piano Sonata and the First Piano Concerto. His Third String Quartet (1927) was awarded the Philadelphia Chamber Music Prize. The Fourth Quartet (1928), the *Cantata Profana* (1930), the Second Piano Concerto, and the Violin Duos (1931) were followed by a period of relative silence which Bartók did, however, devote to arranging folk music.

In 1934 Bartók returned to actual composition with his Fifth Quartet, followed by Twenty-Seven Choruses (1935), Music for Strings, Percussion and Celesta (1936) and the Sonata for Two Pianos and Percussion (1937). In 1937 he also finished his *Mikrokosmos*, a set of 156 piano studies begun eleven years earlier for the benefit of his son Peter. The following year he wrote the Violin Concerto and *Contrasts* for clarinet, violin and piano; this work was especially composed for a trio consisting of Bartók himself, his fellow countryman Szigeti and the jazz clarinetist Benny Goodman. In 1939 came the *Divertimento* for strings and in 1940 his Sixth Quartet.

When war was declared Bartók was in the United States. As he was opposed to Horthy's dictatorship, he decided to remain in America for the duration. He probably counted on his reputation as a pianist and composer to ensure a livelihood for himself and his family. But, despite commissions from the Koussevitsky Foundation—Concerto for Orchestra (1943) —and from Menuhin—Sonata for Unaccompanied Violin (1943–1944)—Bartók's career in wartime America was a dismal failure.

Soon his health declined and he was no longer able even to give recitals. The end of the war brought him new hope, for he was reinstated in the official functions from which he had resigned. It was too late, however; his strength and health had been sapped by years of want, and he died in New York on September 26, 1945, leaving two unfinished scores: a Viola Concerto and the Third Piano Concerto (1945), both of which were completed by his pupil, Tibor Serly. He was buried at the expense of ASCAP.

All those who knew Bartók are unanimous in their description of his character. This remarkably handsome man always acted according to his convictions. He spent the last years of his life in poverty and exile solely because of the courageous stand he had taken during the years of Hitler's triumphs, protesting against the omission of his works from Goebbels' famous exhibition of "degenerate music" in 1936 and, two years later, declaring his solidarity with the Jewish composers in the Universal catalogue when they were banned by the Nazis. His patriotism had an influence on his creative activities, for it was out of love for his native country that he devoted much of his time to a passionate study of Hungarian folk music, publishing several books on the subject. He made considerable use of folk music in his own works, by direct quotation, stylized transposition, and sometimes even purely imaginative *pastiche*.

Symphonic and Chamber Music

We may disregard Bartók's vocal music entirely—he wrote relatively little and it was not a field in which he excelled—and devote all our attention instead to the most significant aspects of his work: the symphonic and chamber music.

In examining his orchestral works we must be careful to distinguish between those which date from before the first World War and those composed after the armistice. Bartók's early work is quite insignificant; it took him some time to free himself from the outside influences—many of them really harmful—that tainted his very first works. The *Portraits* often degenerate into a fake lyricism hardly worthy of Rachmaninoff, while the *Images* derive from a misguided conception of musical impressionism. These two scores were much weaker, both technically and aesthetically, than the First Quartet written at about the same time.

His first important orchestral work was a ballet, *The Miraculous Mandarin*, which also exists in a concert version. This score was undeniably influenced by *The Rite of Spring*, which had had its première only a few years before. Bartók took as raw material the same vertical, dissonant, almost static note-clusters, and brought them to life using similar conflicting rhythms and displaced accents. It would be a grave mistake to rank *The Miraculous Mandarin* on a level with *The Rite of Spring;* still, Bartók's ballet is splendidly orchestrated and contains many fine passages; the finale, in particular, manages to weave a truly feverish spell, with its throbbing, persistent rhythmic patterns.

The Dance Suite, the Rumanian Folk Dances, the Violin Rhapsodies, and the *Divertimento* are the portion of Bartók's orchestral music utilizing actual or imitation folk tunes. They are simple, extremely pleasant works, but completely lacking in depth. More significant, though less sustained and less perfect, are his piano concertos (with the exception of the Third, the banality of which is inexplicable and disturbing). The Second Piano Concerto has neither the profound formal unity nor even the stylistic unity of a masterpiece; but, bracketed by Stravinsky-like first and last movements, it does contain a splendidly expansive Andante which is a truly miraculous achievement in the obscure realm of musical poetics. The interplay of piano, percussion, and strings as they develop a *pianissimo* counterpoint in superposed fifths attains a serene ecstasy almost comparable in its intensity to the "Mystic Circle of the Adolescents" in *The Rite of Spring.* And yet, like every work or page in which Bartók really hit his stride, this Andante bears such an original, personal stamp that it is impossible to ascribe it to any outside influence whatever.

A similar assessment of either the Violin Concerto or the Concerto for Orchestra would be quite impossible; Bartók was starting to age when he wrote these works, and though they are his most famous, they do not rank among his best artistic achievements. His Violin Concerto has often been compared with Berg's, and like Berg's it is an attempt to resolve the conflict that arises when pure chromaticism is incorporated into the tonal system; its lyrical qualitites do not make up for a certain academic stiltedness. In the Concerto for Orchestra, Bartók used his undeniable skill as an orchestrator to convey rather feeble musical ideas and a heterogeneous style which alternately recalls Stravinsky's *Firebird* and Hindemith's *Mathis der Mahler.*

His Music for Strings, Percussion and Celesta, on the other hand, is not only the high point of Bartók's music, it is aesthetically one of the least controvertible scores written between the two World Wars. Considering that it was conceived as a chamber work, the instrumental forces employed are relatively large: a double string orchestra, piano, harp, xylophone, celesta, and percussion section with tympani. The work is a kind of four-movement symphony in cyclical form. The main theme is built on eight of the twelve notes; it is first stated as the subject of a fugue, and together with the "head" of the answer, contains the elements, not of a twelve-tone row, as certain notes are repeated, but of a total chromatic (Fig. 9).

The opening fugue is developed according to a very simple pattern. Each new entry of the subject is placed a fifth higher than the last for the even-numbered entries and a fifth lower for the odd. This two-fold progression begins on the note A—which is not the key of this essentially non-tonal movement, but rather its "axis"—and finally converges on an E-flat at the end of a long crescendo. The second part of the

FIG. 9*

fugue works its way back to the starting point through successive statements of the inverted subject. The second movement, written in the key of C, is in bi-thematic sonata form; its second exposition contains some interesting rhythmic variations on the first. The work's climactic movement is its third, not so much on account of its structure (an ABCBA rondo) as of its great poetic intensity. Bartók's masterful handling of the xylophone and celesta in this movement has seldom been equalled. The A-major finale, on the other hand, is rather tame. It is worth noting that the original theme recurs in the second, third, and fourth movements, but merely as reminiscences and not as an integral part of the work's structure. In point of fact, the only real attempt at a cyclical organization occurs in the finale, in the form of a diatonic transformation of the purely chromatic main theme. It is obvious that Bartók's experiment comes dangerously close to eclecticism, and though he did manage to resolve the conflict, one is entitled

FIG. 10a*

to find his solution rather unsatisfactory. Because of these reservations, and despite many lovely passages and brilliant inventions, the work remains imperfect.

Along with the Sonata for Two Pianos and Percussion, the six quartets tower over the rest of Bartok's chamber music. They derive, on the whole, from an aesthetic conception similar to that of Music for Strings, and tackle similar problems. The First Quartet, for example, begins with a fugue whose subject and answer contain between them the twelve notes of the chromatic scale. The Second Quartet is built on a set of melodic structures grouped around Bartók's favorite interval, the diminished fifth. The theme of the second movement, with

FIG. 10b**

its two augmented fourths (Fig. 10a), prefigures a similar pattern in the allegro movement of Music for Strings (Fig. 10b). Similarly, the initial figure of the Third Quartet (Fig. 10c), with its major seconds that double back on themselves—another melodic trait typical of Bartók—recalls the last notes of the subject in the fugue (Fig. 9). (Certain critics maintain that Bartók went through an "expressionistic" period during 1926 and 1927, best typified by the Third Quartet. It is true that in this work Bartók carried to its furthest extremes his fondness for dissonance, giving the music a contorted quality that he heightened by a somewhat excessive use of such external devices as *glissando*, bowing on the bridge and finger-board, *col legno*, and so forth. The work is quite attractive nonetheless, particularly because of its finale, in which the thematic elements of the first movement are recapitulated.) In the Fourth and Fifth Quartets, Bartók's approach to the problem of cycli-

FIG. 10c*

cal construction was more direct than in any of his later works. The Fourth Quartet is based upon a completely symmetrical structure similar to that which he later used in the slow movement of Music for Strings. Here the slow movement acts as a pivot, with the four other movements grouped on either side of it in pairs. The first movement establishes themes and a structure that later recur in the more leisurely atmosphere of the last movement. The second and fourth movements are both scherzos, and their affinities are equally apparent. Another noteworthy similarity with Music for Strings is that the first theme of the fourth movement (*Allegro Pizzicato*) is simply the chromatic theme of the second movement restated in diatonic form. The Fifth Quartet is a much more uneven work. Architecturally less rigorous than the Fourth, it also lacks the earlier work's expressive bite. It is most remarkable for the texture of its writing. The first movement contains another example of the use of a lowered dominant which so often typifies Bartók's tonal conception. Finally, the Sixth Quartet, though undoubtedly less interesting, is nevertheless based upon an original idea: the gradual exposition in one, two, three, and four parts in each of its four movements, of a single theme subjected to various transformations.

It is hard to form an opinion of Bartók's piano music as a whole; its unevenness may be explained—though hardly excused—by the fact that he wrote so much for the instrument. The spirited rhythms of the *Allegro Barbaro* or the all but incoherent violence of the Piano Sonata, both outwardly attractive works, cannot hide their conceptual weaknesses. The *Études,* on the other hand, contain highly respectable rhythmic and stylistic inventions and while the *Mikrokosmos* was a project that stemmed from motives less directly musical than educational, it remains, on this level, very laudable.

It was not until 1937, however, that Bartók wrote his keyboard masterpiece, the Sonata for Two Pianos and Percussion. Though nearly contemporary with Music for Strings, this Sonata contains scarcely a hint of the conflict between tonality and non-tonality which made the earlier work so disturbingly equivocal. It is frankly in the key of C and uses chromaticism as an element of tension. The score's merits are obvious ones: it is very cleverly written and flows in a simple but flawless line; it displays Bartók's brilliant flair for melodic invention and, above all, his amazing mastery of instrumentation coupled with an uncommon rhythmic vivacity. The instrumental problems involved in this work call to mind those faced by Stravinsky in *Les Noces*. Bartók handled them with considerable originality; the percussion parts are alternately set at odds with the two pianos or incorporated into their polyphonic design. At times they merely reinforce the keyboard discourse, while at others they may establish a rhythmic counterpoint or even a theme of their own. In addition, this colorful work achieves a remarkable sense of balance. The composer did an orchestral version, entitled Concerto for Two Pianos.

Characteristics of Bartók's Music

Bartók's music is many-sided, and hard to appraise as a whole. For this reason, a piecemeal approach to it may be the best. Depending upon whether they draw their inspiration from folk music, from Hindemith, or from Schönberg, his melodies may be modal, tonal, or non-tonal. The chromatic and diatonic scales are locked in a permanent struggle, though in the end the latter generally gains the upper hand (as in the finale of Music for Strings). Bartók was in love with dissonance, but the acid harmonic idiom in which he gave vent to this passion was somewhat crude. In general, his contrapuntal combinations "stick fairly close to the half-tone," as Olivier Messiaen puts it. Very few composers have had Bartók's deep, instinctive feeling for the beauty of unresolved dissonance and unpolarized, non-tonal melody. The subject of the fugue in his Music for Strings and the overlapping polyphony derived from it are nearly as beautiful as the finest passages in Schönberg's pre-tone-row compositions. However, it is important to realize that with Bartók the word *dissonance* still has real meaning, and his superpositions of seconds and sevenths do not produce the same neutral coloring and uniform density as in the music of Webern, for example. In this respect, Bartók, despite his modernity, remains a composer of the past.

Nor do Bartók's rhythmic concepts have the cohesiveness or the active structural functions of those elaborated by Stravinsky in *The Rite of Spring*. Often, however, he did manage to derive a great variety of lively rhythms from folk music; rhythm was the chief outlet for his violent temperament, and he has been said to have transformed his piano into a veritable armored tank. Accents play an important role in his music, and his approach to them was particularly original, constituting, in fact, a minor—though by no means negligible—aspect of the revolution in rhythm which has characterized twentieth-century European music.

Bartók also displayed an evident concern for form which, at its best, resulted in the partial rejuvenation of a traditional structure (the fugue in Music for Strings). More often, however, he was satisfied with classical molds, and especially with the sonata form. His developments almost always take the shape of canonic imitation. Despite this structural rigidity, however, Bartók's musical ideas are extremely fluid and would be attractively ambiguous were it not for their lack of rigor; the fact is that whenever Bartók did manage to avoid archaic formal types, he fell into the hackneyed error of partitioned structures, thereby condemning his forms to a compartmentalization which is not enough to save them from anarchy.[1]

Above all, Bartók was a great orchestrator. This is the field in which he displayed the full extent of his gifts; witness his mastery of instrumental problems and his flair for sumptuous color. True, his notions on instrumentation were less pure, less intimately related to form than those of Webern or even Schönberg; but in the alchemy of tone-color he attained, at times, a degree of poetic intensity worthy of a master; one is reminded of Schönberg's Five Pieces and occasionally even of *The Rite of Spring.*

---

[1] I should point out that Bartók (like Honegger and a number of other composers concerned with the rejuvenation of set forms) attempted to apply to music certain principles borrowed from architecture. Thus certain symmetrical relationships inherited from classical builders and astute (or naive) transpositions of "the golden rule" came to play a role in musical composition. The reason why this innovation has had no startling effects is that it derives from a misconception. Our perception of time cannot conceivably be subjected to the laws governing our perception of volume. Moreover, formal restraints of this sort, which do not stem from the requirements of musical material *per se* but are grafted onto it from without, restore to composition that predestined quality which Debussy did away with long ago. At best a solution of this kind can be regarded only as a temporary reprieve.

All in all, it is very difficult to judge a composer whose music is so disconcertingly uneven. Though very prolific, he produced only a handful of memorable scores, ten at the very most. Are these enough to allow us to define Bartók's place in musical history? But then how many more works from the pen of his famous compatriot, Franz Liszt, have survived the test of time?

Bartók borrowed a great deal from nearly every other great composer of his day, with the sole exception of Webern, whose music he might just as well never have heard. He did, however, acquire a thorough mastery and understanding of the material borrowed thus, and managed, at times, to blend it effectively with his own music, stamping it with the mark of his personal genius. His importance lies more, perhaps, in his powers of synthesis than in his actual inventiveness. Immediately after his death, it was possible to regard him as the precursor of a new classicism; almost every composer who did not choose to follow Webern looked to Bartók for guidance. As we shall see, however, postwar music has proven that he was on the wrong track. Bartók's decline in his later years, which were so similar in this respect to those of Schönberg, Berg, and Stravinsky, together with the uncertainty and even downright mediocrity of his very last works, scarcely allows us to cast him in a role denied the other three. Today it is an easy matter to avoid any such confusion of values, but one may even wonder whether the above-mentioned name of Liszt will not one day outweigh that of Bartók in the history of Hungarian music.

Part Two

Béla Bartók was the last valid representative of a certain classical-romantic tradition which, to all intents and purposes, vanished with the Hungarian master. The following generation of composers—men who came of age between 1920 and 1940—was a "doomed" generation, in the cruelest sense of the term. Never since the Middle Ages has music known such a barren period. A great deal of courage and exceptional gifts would have been required to replant the scorched earth which the great destroyers had left in their wake; as it happened, nearly every composer eluded this historical challenge and found refuge in a travesty of aesthetic values. At a time when the music of the great modern masters was on the decline, that of their disciples and successors, now automatically promoted to the rank of masters, attested only to their confusion or self-complacency. Even standards of craftsmanship were fast being debased by a vogue of amateurism. A postwar composer has coined the most ferocious definition of that generation's collective cowardice, "a generation," he says, "composed chiefly of militant illiterates."

Thanks to immensely gifted performers, perhaps the greatest it had ever known, tonal music seemed at the height of its glory; yet actually its time had already run out, and nothing was left for it but to recede slowly into the past. One wonders whether it will ever again be served by musicians of the caliber of Flagstad, Fischer, Furtwängler, or Walter. But, at that very time, what was happening to the art these musicians were glorifying, the art which had produced the B Minor Mass and Beethoven's Ninth Symphony? Was the tiny, flickering flame of Webern's late works its only sign of life?

In the midst of that doomed generation, a very small number of distinguished composers preserved sufficient integrity to reject the so-called "ésthétique du music-hall" and other facile solutions that were all too easily accepted by most of their contemporaries. Did they realize that their impassioned quest for new aesthetic incentives would inevitably lead to the most agonizing failure? For this, it would seem, was the tragic destiny of those artists so strangely sacrificed by history; the career of Olivier Messiaen, who stands at the forefront of his generation, is largely symbolic of these composers' fate.

Igor Stravinsky

Arnold Schönberg

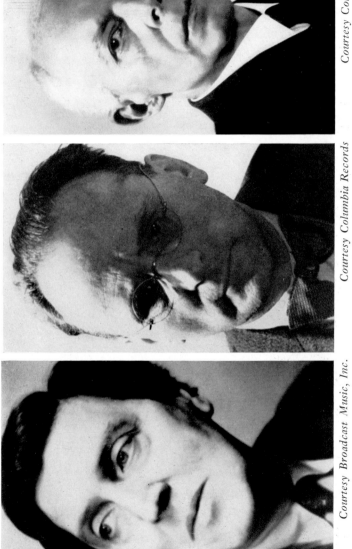

Alban Berg

Anton Webern

Béla Bartók

Olivier Messiaen

Photo-Ingi

Pierre Boulez

David Tudor

Ferdinand Boes

Edgar Varèse

Fred Plaut

Karlheinz Stockhausen

Photo-Lipni

Jean Barraqué

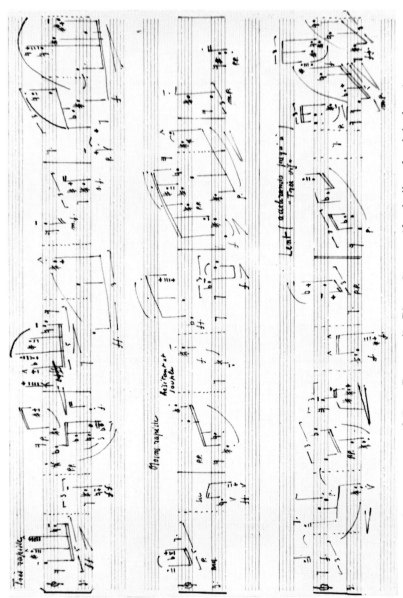

First measures of Jean Barraqué's Piano Sonata (facsimile of original ms.)

CHAPTER SIX

Olivier Messiaen

Messiaen's Career

Olivier Messiaen was born in Avignon on December 10, 1908. His mother was the poet Cécile Sauvage and his father an eminent scholar of English. He lived for a time in Grenoble, and there began studying the piano on his own. As a child, he was already interested in composition, and when he entered the Paris Conservatory in 1919, he was naturally drawn to the classes in harmony and counterpoint. During the ten years he spent in that institution, studying with the Gallon brothers, Caussade, Estyle, Dupré, Emmanuel, and Dukas, he won five first prizes in five different subject matters: fugue and counterpoint, accompaniment, organ and improvisation, history of music, and composition.

His first published score was an organ piece entitled *Le Ban-*

quet Céleste (1928). The following year, Messiaen wrote a rather long set of Préludes for the piano. In 1930 he wrote his first orchestral work, *Les Offrandes Oubliées,* which was also the only symphonic work of his to be performed prior to the second World War. It was followed in 1932 by the *Fantaisie Burlesque* for piano, the Theme and Variations for piano and violin, and an organ work whose title—*Apparition de l'Église Éternelle*—reflects Messiaen's deep-felt desire to express Christian mysticism through poetry and music. The young composer had just been appointed organist at the church of La Trinité. His efforts to reform church music gave rise to a certain amount of friction with the parish authorities; but though a soft-spoken man, Messiaen is also very stubborn, and he finally had his way; as a result, a few non-Catholics came to the church every Sunday to hear improvisations which did not always meet with the approval of the congregation.

In 1933, Messiaen composed his first major work, *l'Ascension,* a set of four symphonic meditations. They were not performed in their orchestral version until 1945, under the baton of Charles Münch. But in 1934, Messiaen did an organ transcription of the work. *L'Ascension* lasts over half an hour, but his next work, *La Nativité du Seigneur* (1935), also for organ, was conceived on an even larger scale. A society called *Les Amis de l'Orgue* was responsible for giving the work its first performance in the church of La Trinité; three of Messiaen's former school-fellows, Jean Langlais, Jean-Jacques Grunenwald, and Daniel Lesur each played three of the work's nine sections. In 1936, Messiaen joined Lesur, André Jolivet, and Yves Baudrier in founding an *avant-garde* group which took the name of "Jeune France." At that time, Messiaen already displayed a strong pedagogical bent which led him, apparently despite his inward repugnance, to come to terms with Parisian musical circles and institutions; that same year he was invited to teach at the École Normale de Musique and at the

Scola Cantorum, stronghold of those most formidable of all French traditionalists, the disciples of Vincent d'Indy.

Until the eve of the second World War, Messiaen's vocal music had been confined to a few little songs. Only then did he begin to write seriously for the voice, composing *Poèmes pour Mi* and *Les Chants de la Terre et du Ciel*. For both these works, the composer wrote his own verse. The first-named work dates from 1936 and was orchestrated the following year; the second dates from 1938. The last work written by Messiaen before his mobilization was a set of seven organ pieces called *Les Corps Glorieux* (1939). Messiaen was captured by the Germans in 1940, and while still in a *stalag* composed the *Quatuor pour la Fin du Temps* (1941); he himself gave the first performance of the work with the help of other musicians among his fellow prisoners. Liberated in 1941, he was almost immediately appointed professor of harmony at the Conservatory, on the recommendation of Marcel Dupré. He thus became the youngest member of the staff of that venerable institution, and his teachings were to seem somewhat revolutionary. The war years were also Messiaen's most prolific period: *Les Sept Visions d'Amen,* for two pianos, was written in 1943 while *Les Vingt Regards sur l'Enfant Jésus*, his longest work to date (two and one half hours), dates from 1944. That same year he wrote *Les Trois Petites Liturgies de la Présence Divine,* for chorus, piano, Ondes Martenot (an electronic instrument developed by Maurice Martenot), and orchestra. Most of these works were dedicated to the young pianist Yvonne Loriod, in whom Messiaen says he has found the perfect exponent of his music. These works enjoyed an immediate success, and at the age of thirty-five Messiaen's reputation, previously very limited, suddenly reached world-wide proportions.

Immediately after the war, Messiaen composed three *Talas* for piano, Ondes Martenot, and large orchestra, which created quite a scandal at the Paris première. Later they became three of the ten movements of his *Turangalîla Symphonie* (1946–1948), commissioned by the Koussevitsky Foundation and given its world première by the Boston Symphony Orchestra, conducted by Leonard Bernstein. In the catalogue of the composer's complete works, *Turangalîla* is preceded and followed by two smaller works that are related to it: *Harawi*, for voice and piano (1945) and *Cinq Rechants* for mixed chorus (1949); the latter was the last work belonging to what is generally regarded as Messiaen's "first period."

Indeed, beginning in 1949, the composer seemed to feel, by "ricochet," the influence of his own teachings which, as it turned out, had not fallen on deaf ears. While continuing to give his Conservatory course in harmony, Messiaen had organized a private course in musical analysis, aesthetics, and rhythm; in 1947 he was asked to give this course at the Conservatory (though he was deemed too young—and probably too dangerous—to be granted a full professorship in composition there). Some of the finest composers and musicians of the next generation—Yvette Grimaud, Yvonne Loriod, Jean Barraqué, Serge Nigg, Michel Fano, Karel Goyewaerts, Karlheinz Stockhausen and Pierre Boulez—attended these classes and heard Messiaen expound his analysis of *The Rite of Spring* and, above all, his carefully reasoned analysis of *Pelleas*, of which he would sing all the roles in his timid voice. The influence of Boulez, who had so brilliantly succeeded in reorganizing and enlarging the world of row music—a form of music which, until then had been rather foreign to the composer of the *Petites Liturgies*—was beginning to have a revolutionary effect on Parisian musical circles, and it was undoubtedly this influence which temporarily steered Messiaen toward a more abstract conception of music. This new direction was expressed in four *Études de Rhythme* for piano: *Mode de Valeurs et d'Intensités*; *Neumes Rhythmiques* (1949) and *Ile de Feu I* and *II* (1950), as well as in *La Messe de Pentecôte* (1950) and *Le Livre d'Orgue* (1951). In 1952, Messiaen took a stab at "musique concrète" with a

work called *Timbres-Durées*. But his attempt to enter into the
mainstream of contemporary musical activities was short-lived.
Subsequently, the composer seemed to feel he had found his
path in a kind of "back to nature" attitude. For years he had
been patiently writing down bird calls, and occasionally incorporating them, in stylized form, into his works. Around
1953, however, bird calls became the basic material of his
music, as is shown by the titles of all his recent scores: *Le
Réveil des Oiseaux*, for piano and orchestra (1953), *Oiseaux
Exotiques*, for piano and wind instruments (1955–1956) and
Premier Catalogue d'Oiseaux, for piano (1957–1958).

Aside from his teaching and composing activities, Messiaen
occasionally takes part in performances of his piano works,
playing the *Études de Rhythme* or the second piano part in the
Visions d'Amen; similarly, Messiaen the organist quite rightly
confines himself to interpreting his own music for this instrument and has now done a recording of his complete organ
works which is, of course, definitive. The world première of
his *Livre d'Orgue*, given at a Domaine Musical concert on
March 21, 1955, was considered by Paris music lovers as one
of the more noteworthy postwar musical events. It enabled
Messiaen to gauge his popularity as a composer which, though it
cannot compare with that of Poulenc, for example, does have
the merit of stemming from a more demanding attitude toward
the public. Messiaen's importance, both as a composer and a
teacher, was emphasized in the tribute paid him by the German review *Melos* on his fiftieth birthday; his three most important pupils, Boulez, Stockhausen, and Barraqué all contributed to this issue. Jean Barraqué wrote:

> The student who has been desiccated by all the arbitrary
> rules met with in other courses, often comes to Messiaen's
> classroom with the naive hope that the secrets of some mirac-
> ulously simple recipe will be revealed to him there. He for-
> gets that a great teacher brings nothing to his pupils, he
> merely provokes them. Messiaen has carefully avoided es-

tablishing the theoretical method of analysis that some would like to see him lay down. Only the works themselves matter, radiant in their devastating splendor. He looks upon each work as a fresh mystery and tackles it with his own resources. Those with other resources are free to make different discoveries. This was the basis of their stringent apprenticeship in a kind of intuitive musical insight. The most striking thing about Messiaen, above and beyond the literal content of his teachings, is his deep-felt, wholehearted love of music. It may seem absurd to marvel at a composer's unselfish fondness for his art. And yet this requires a tremendous capacity for solitude and silence; only the elite among composers know how to keep silent the better to hear. Most of them are too anxious to compose. Messiaen impressed us, his pupils, as a teacher who knew how to keep still and listen. What agonizing experience must a man have undergone to retain that attitude of respectful humility before the works of others, considering them not as frozen in a splendid, remote past, but as acting out their own lives and deaths with their own self-contained energy.

Messiaen: A Self-Portrait

"It is always dangerous to talk about oneself," writes Messiaen at the beginning of his book *Technique de mon Langage Musical* (1942–1944). And yet few composers have shown so little modesty in commenting upon their own music. Such a degree of complacency—he has even been accused of exhibitionism—can only derive either from an extraordinary naiveté, or from the firm conviction that one is in possession of unique truth; in Messiaen's case, both hypotheses may be corret. Still, the self-portrait found between the lines of the commentaries which he has appended to music of which he seems passionately fond, may enable us to appraise it more fairly.

Messiaen is an unusual man, a figure apart, whose thinking nevertheless paradoxically contains a mixture of ideas, all of which had a certain influence on the generation he represents. His cultural background is almost exclusively Catholic (his favorite authors are Pierre Reverdy, Ernest Hello, T. S. Eliot, and Dom Columba Marmion) and has made him a man of tradition; but his mind is hungry for novelty and rebels against academic routine. This devout composer's ideal is "a *true* music, that is to say a spiritual music, one which is an act of faith; a music which touches on every subject and yet remains in constant touch with God; then, too, an original music, whose language may open a few new doors and pluck off a few, still distant stars." Messiaen does not feel that a respect for tradition need rule out innovation. In his eyes, the values of the past—read Christian values—are subject to a never-ending process of growth.

All his music reflects this basic pre-disposition. "Melody first and foremost!" proclaims Messiaen. "Melody was the starting-point, long may it reign!—and no matter how complex our rhythms and harmonies, these shall never drag melody in their wake, but, on the contrary, obey it as devoted slaves; harmony, most particularly, shall always remain 'natural,' for it lies latent in melody and has stemmed from it since the dawn of time." This hierarchical conception of music goes hand in hand with a basically conservative attitude toward form. "We shall not reject the old rules of harmony and form. Never lose sight of them," he writes, but then immediately adds: "either cleaving strictly to them, enlarging upon them, or completing them with even older rules—or with new ones." Thus, though Messiaen is a conservative, he is not a reactionary: he seems to be more concerned with actively carrying on tradition than with passively defending it.

Messiaen is a descendant of Chopin and Debussy in that he lays stress on the sensuous side of music. "Our goal," he says, "is an iridescent music, one which will delight the auditory senses with delicate, voluptuous pleasures." To his mind, "the listener's only desire is to be charmed. And," he adds, "this is precisely what will occur: he will succumb, in spite of himself, to the strange charm of impossibilities: a certain effect of tonal ubiquity . . . and a certain unity of motion . . . will lead him gently towards that *theological rainbow* which is the ultimate goal of the music we are seeking to build in both theory and practice." This attempt to humanize music does not take the form of expressionistic devices such as those made fashionable by Berg and Bartók—far from it. With Messiaen it remains an integral part of the written texture of his music. Though Messiaen the organist is past master in the alchemy of tone-colors, he tends to favor harmony as the vehicle for expressing this humanistic dimension. "Natural harmony, the one true harmony, voluptuously pretty in its essence . . ." is prescribed by him as a vital condition for any authentic approach to polyphony. However, this concern with sensuous pleasure is inseparably linked, in Messiaen's mind, with the "lofty sentiments" which music should convey ("and in particular, the loftiest of all, the religious sentiments exalted by the theology and truths of our Catholic faith").

Just what is that *strange charm of impossibilities* with which Messiaen claims to solve the apparently insoluble equation propounded by an art which would be at once thoroughly sensuous and in touch with the highest form of spirituality? "This charm, both voluptuous and contemplative, resides especially in certain mathematical impossibilities in the domains of mode and rhythm: the number of transpositions of a mode are limited, since the notes ultimately repeat themselves, and there are rhythms which cannot be retrograded because the order of the time-values remains unchanged; these are two prominent examples of impossibility." Modes, rhythms, transpositions, retrogradations, there is no doubt but what Messiaen intends to elaborate the musical poetics thus defined on a technical basis.

Messiaen's Reform of Musical Language

Messiaen is unquestionably an accomplished harmonist; he has gone as far as it seems possible to go in the rejuvenation of organ music, and has displayed his gifts as an orchestrator in more than one work. Yet his real discoveries were made in the field of rhythm, and he himself has always been conscious of this fact. A catalogue of his works, published after the war with the composer's approval, introduces him as "composer *and rhythmatician.*" By this curious appendage the composer of the *Harawi* meant to distinguish himself from other composers who, at that time, were fairly indifferent to the problems of rhythmic organization; on the fourth page of the catalogue, a footnote made this absolutely clear: "What sets him entirely apart from the rest of contemporary music is his new approach to rhythm."

"We are indebted to Messiaen," writes Pierre Boulez, "for having created a conscious technique of duration, based upon his thorough studies of plain-chant, Hindu rhythm, and the music of Stravinsky. This was undoubtedly an important contribution, since—aside from the bootless habit of trying to reconstitute Greek meter that crops up now and again—one must go as far back as the fourteenth century to find a similar concern among Western composers (whereas it was a constant factor in the music of other civilizations—Africa, India, Bali, and Java)."[1] Messiaen may be regarded as Western music's first great theoretician of rhythm, and his influence in this domain has already borne fruit. His famous analysis of *The Rite of Spring* laid the groundwork for Boulez's own analysis, more thorough and better motivated. The opening chapters of *Technique de mon Langage Musical*, which prefigured his subsequent *Traité de Rhythme*, were full of original insights. In his classes, Messiaen has always stressed the rhythmic aspect of

---

[1] P. Boulez: "Eventuellement," in *La Revue Musicale*, April, 1952.

the classical and modern works offered for the contemplation of his students; this constitutes an important contribution to modern methods of musical education.

Like Stravinsky, Messiaen rejects metrical unity, even measures, and the regular alternation of strong-beats and off-beats; he has replaced these notions with an "unmeasured" meter based on "an intuitive feeling for a given short value and its unhampered multiplication." This was the first step in a gradual liberation of rhythm, in the course of which Messiaen devised such daring technical solutions as the notion of beats of unequal duration. Having thus abolished the tyranny of the bar-

FIG. 11

a) **Non-retrograde** rhythm: remains unchanged whether it be read backwards or forwards.

b) Asymmetrical enlargement of a rhythmic cell; according to the usual rules of augmentation, the last note should be a dotted quarter.

c) Added value (vertical arrow).

line, Messiaen set about strengthening the sub-structure of his music by introducing rhythms derived from Hindu *decitalas*. He generally builds these rhythms on primary numbers (5, 7, 11, and 13) and in order to vary a given rhythm, will use more complex methods than the usual augmentations and diminutions: simple asymmetry, *added time-values* (added units, rests, or, occasionally, a dot added to one of the rhythmic cell's component notes). His rhythms are often non-retrograde, that is to say symmetrical with respect to a fixed, central time value (Fig. 11).

These two concepts—non-retrograde rhythm and added

time-value—do not, at first glance, seem very compatible. The former is the ideal expression of a symmetrical order which the latter seems destined to combat. Messiaen makes no effort to reconcile these two conflicting concepts. Though he occasionally toys with asymmetrical structures, he is a staunch advocate of the notion that formal equilibrium implies symmetry, and in actual practice considerably limits the scope of action of the added value. Instead of working toward the concept of "irrational" rhythm later invented by his pupils, he continued to look upon the adjunct merely as an element of conflict within the regular meter, an additional dash of charm which he calls "a wee-bit perverse" because it gives the rhythm a "delightfully halting quality," in other words, as the spice indispensable to any decadent music. I am not the first to have observed that even when the added value is incorporated into its rhythmic structures, a Messiaen score often sounds like one long *rubato*.

Another, more general conception is predominant in Messiaen's rhythmic idiom, that of *isorhythm;* it takes two complementary forms in his work: the *ostinato*—which he calls "rhythmic pedal-point"—and the rhythmic canon. Musicians call *isorhythm* the application of a single rhythmic pattern to several different melodic patterns. Thus canonic imitation and persistent repetitions act upon the time-value of each note, independently of its height or depth, and the rhythmic texture is dissociated from the polyphonic texture. This was the "point of departure," as Boulez himself calls it, for a conception which the next generation was to develop along more revolutionary lines. In Messiaen's music, this revival of isorhythm led to nothing more than a rather stilted polyrhythmic idiom which avoids the flexibility afforded by the irrational time-value, and the components of which are conceived to fit easily—too easily, one feels—into huge superpositions resting on stable, highly simplified variation-principles: rhythmic canons obtained through augmentations by fractional values, rhythmic pedal-points the components of which are gradually eliminated, etc. (Fig. 12a and 12b).

FIG. 12a*

Polyrhythm and polymodality

Line (a) contains an *ostinato* repetition of an eight-note rhythm of which line (b) contains the strict retrograde. This retrograde, also treated "in *ostinato*," is displaced by the value of an eighth-rest with each new repetition. Line (c) contains a repeated, nine-note non-retrograde rhythm centered about a dotted eighth note.

These three "*rhythmic pedal-points*" are superposed to form a complex polyrhythmic structure which is associated in turn with a complex polymodal structure: the harmonic and melodic notes (a′) of the melody which corresponds to (a) belong to the Second Mode of Limited Transpositions; (b) is in the Third Mode (b′); (c), which has no harmonic accompaniment, is in the First Mode.

FIG. 12b**

The rhythmic canon exists independently of any melodic canon. In this example, the chords on the upper staff belong to the Second Mode, those of the lower to the Third Mode.

---

* Olivier Messiaen, *L'Ange aux Parfums.* Reprinted by permission of Alphonse Leduc, Paris.

** Olivier Messiaen, *Epouvante.* Reprinted by permission of Durand & Co., Paris.

This rhythmic architecture undoubtedly engenders a good deal of waste. In certain parts of the *Turangalîla Symphonie*, for example, the permutations involving primary numbers that are both too large and too close to one another to be detected by the unaided ear constitute little more than an intellectual exercise. In this same work, the use of "rhythmic characters"—inspired by *The Rite of Spring*—which Messiaen would have the listeners follow as they thread their way through shameless melodic effusions that are entirely foreign to the rhythmic action, seems an utterly gratuitous device (unless it is the inadequate expression of more obscure intentions). The naively morbid delight which Messiaen took in juxtaposing and interchanging sonorities and time-values in his "monodic" *Timbres-Durées*, which lasts no less than seventeen minutes, seems to betoken a complete lack of self-control.

These reservations, however, are minor when one considers the extent of Messiaen's accomplishment. His major contribution is two-fold: he "enlarged the scope of the tension-relaxation principle by means of the three-fold group, *anacrusis-accent-termination*"—which laid the groundwork for the most recent concepts of rhythm—and he invented the modes of time-values, attacks, and intensities, which prefigured Boulez's "all-encompassing" serial organization. For it is in the *Études de Rhythme* that Messiaen offers the most absorbing—albeit fortuitous—aspect of his music; in this work he was a true precursor. Actually, he did not invent a new concept so much as foreshadow its invention. This may simply have been because he lacked a clear, decisive insight into the musical universe about to be born; he was far too involved with the past to envisage, in all its devastating rigor, the revolution he was unwittingly helping to prepare.

Messiaen the "rhythmatician" remains one of the seminal forces behind contemporary musical thought. "We are indebted to him," acknowledged Pierre Boulez, "for his attempt to set up a dialectic of duration by experimenting with hierarchies of note-values (variable contrasts between relatively short and relatively long time-values, which may in turn be either odd or even), a dialectic which in itself provides a means of musical development when it acts upon the structures of rhythmic neumes."[2] As a polyphonist, Messiaen unfortunately proved less audacious. The solutions he advocated—twenty years after Webern!—came much too late. They tended to enlarge the scope of modes that were first used by the Russians and further explored by Debussy. Hindu tradition had taught him that it was possible to derive *modes* from the total chromatic, possible, that is, to set up defective chromatic scales. Taking as his point of departure the seventy-two Hindu modes gravitating about those perennial cornerstones the tonic and

FIG. 13

the dominant, Messiaen established seven scales of his own, called "scales of limited transposition." The simplest of these scales, which he calls the "first mode," is simply the whole-tone scale obtained by superposing two augmented fifth chords at the interval of a major second; this mode can be transposed only once (Fig. 13).[3]

It plays only a very small role in Messiaen's music; "Claude Debussy and later Paul Dukas used it to such remarkable effect that they exhausted its possibilities. We shall therefore be careful to avoid using it unless it can be concealed in a group of superposed modes so as to be unrecognizable" (cf. Fig. 12a). The "second mode," on the other hand, is a more original in-

----

[2] P. Boulez: "Eventuellement."

[3] Messiaen says it "may be transposed twice." I feel it is more logical not to count the original state of the mode. Thus, I consider the diatonic scale transposable eleven times, not twelve.

vention, and Messiaen makes extensive use of it. This mode employs two-thirds of the total chromatic rather than half of it; the notes are alternately separated by half-tones and whole-tones. The mode as a whole is obtained by superposing two diminished seventh chords with the interval of a minor second between them; like its component chords, it may be transposed twice (Fig. 14).

FIG. 14

Like the classical major scale, this mode is internally symmetrical; its component cells are all alike. This feature, which is common to all scales of limited transposition, recurs in a slightly modified form in Messiaen's "third mode," which comprises three-fourths of the notes in the total chromatic separated successively by a whole tone, a half tone, a half tone, etc. The resulting scale corresponds to the superposition of three augmented fifth chords, and can be transposed three times (Fig. 15).

FIG. 15

Finally, Messiaen recognizes the existence of four other modes, centered around the augmented fourth and, like it, transposable five times; he considers these modes less interesting "precisely because they have too many transpositions."

All of these modes can modulate within themselves (from one transposition to another), modulate from one mode to another, or be related to a major scale "by the frequent recurrence of the tonic of a selected key or the utilization of this key's dominant seventh"; they may also be related to—or contrasted with—Greek, Chinese, or Hindu modes. According to Messiaen, they allow for polymodality (cf. Fig. 12a) but not polytonality: "The chords and note-combinations to which they give rise may, at times, resemble polytonal sonorities, but they will always be re-absorbed by the power of the mode."

This "modal power," however, is often forced to abdicate in favor of the greater tonal strength contained in the tonic-dominant relationship. It is doubtful whether the mode of limited transpositions can counteract the impression of tonality for more than a few seconds, and in fact tonality asserts itself in all of Messiaen's major works. Despite his lavish use of appoggiatura and "added notes" (augmented fourths, added sixths) with which he hopes to obtain the "variegated" and "stained window" effects that he cherishes, his harmony is constantly acknowledging the ties that bind it to tonality. Still more serious, however, is the fact that Messiaen's modes seem to grow "old" before their time, while the major and minor scales did not. As he himself has observed in connection with the whole-tone scale, it would seem that far from opening up fresh perspectives, the repeated use of these scales exhausts their possibilities and drains their powers of development.

Though he tends to disregard performing difficulties, Messiaen's instrumental writing does have its internal consistency. Its goal, however, is generally sumptuosity rather than economy of means. As an organ composer, Messiaen's inventiveness has enabled him to avoid the academic formalism of his teacher, Dupré, and beneath his finger tips, the organ has a new sound for the first time since Franck; but then this may merely be the swan song of a once glorious instrument. In any case, Messiaen is so accustomed to the organ that at times his orchestral writing seems to be a symphonic projection of an idea originally conceived as a registration. I do not mean to question Messiaen's mastery of instrumentation; never has the Ondes Martenot been as perfectly incorporated into the orchestra as in his *Petites*

Liturgies, and he is the first composer to have made proper use of the vibraphone. Rather, his weaknesses stem from the heart of his aesthetic conceptions: his excessively linear use of tone-color (a concept which was already implicitly superseded by the orchestral fabric of Debussy's *Jeux*) and his fondness for overloaded orchestration, probably a post-Wagnerian rather than a Wagnerian legacy. His piano idiom has revived the "grand piano" style created by Beethoven in his late sonatas and further developed by Liszt and Ravel; it is sometimes very felicitous, as is always the case when Messiaen is dealing with purely aural phenomena: his individualization of registers and his "chord-clusters" display a highly developed aural sensitivity. Though it is an obvious exaggeration to consider Messiaen as the "inventor of the modern piano"—as Yvonne Loriod once wrote—his influence in this respect on such works as Stockhausen's *Klavierstücke* and Boulez's Third Sonata is undeniable.

Messiaen's Downfall: Form

There are two main tendencies in Messiaen's music; the one involves non-retrograde rhythms, added time-values, rhythmic pedal-point and rhythmic canons, all of which tend toward a polyrhythmic conception of musical discourse, while the other involves modes of limited transposition, added notes, pedal groups and superpositions which converge toward polymodality. The analogy between these two tendencies is clear and their correlation is part of Messiaen's intentions: "the modes of limited transposition," he writes, "will accomplish vertically (transposition) what the non-retrograde rhythms accomplish horizontally (retrogradation)." Defined in this way, Messiaen's musical idiom takes on a certain overall coherence. Melody is supreme and although harmony may undergo an infinite variety of subtle refinements, it remains subordinated to melody through the modes. He has conducted a vigorous reappraisal of rhythm in his music, and this element does tend to free itself from melody and assume a structural function. Tone-color and dynamics, highlighted by a written texture which is often quite complex, serve to prolong effects obtained through the use of modes and rhythms. But topping it all off we find, of course, the eminently traditional notions of theme, symmetry, and continuity.

This is undoubtedly the source of the contradictions which ultimately pervaded Messiaen's music and stifled his creative powers. In his attempt to overhaul musical idiom, this eminent technician, this extraordinarily keen-eared harmonist, this erudite and discerning analyst was defeated by that obstacle which has been the stumbling block of every composer since Debussy: *form*. In this domain, Messiaen has proven completely—and, I fear, definitively—impotent. His painstakingly elaborated modes and rhythms have produced a musical edifice which is attractive and colorful but which rests on poverty-stricken, outmoded structures. Contrary to Messiaen's expectations, the "charm of impossibilities," far from creating "a certain effect of tonal ubiquity" and "a certain unity of motion (in which the end and the beginning meet in an absolute identity)" produces little more than a sense of monotony and inertia, once the listener has recovered from the often pleasant surprise of a first hearing. For it soon becomes apparent that the most anachronistic aspect of Messiaen's music is its ultra-static character.

The greatest Western music—Bach's great organ chorales, Beethoven's Fifteenth Quartet—has taught us that the highest forms of musical expression stem from that miraculous phenomenon, "evolutive contemplation." Messiaen, taking his cue from Far Eastern tradition, reduces the musical phenomenon to a kind of frozen contemplation, incapable of any internal development. This alarming step backwards is implicit in every one of his notions on music. The non-retrograde rhythms contribute strongly to this static quality, but the chain forged by the modes of limited transpositions is an even more powerful factor. Speculating on the specious idea that "a repeat is the same as a hold," Messiaen has invented the "pedal-group" which further inhibits motion in his music (two hundred years earlier, J. S. Bach had already transformed pedal-point into a dynamic repose). Surely this is a sign of Messiaen's willful immobility which, to my mind, is a flimsy mask to conceal his lack of formal inventiveness.

There were many signs pointing to Messiaen's ultimate failure as a composer. I have already referred to the contradiction inherent in his attitude of "enlightened conservatism"; though too enlightened to be content, like the neo-classicists, with the formal clichés of old, he was still too tradition-conscious to reconsider music as a whole, at a point in history when the achievements of Debussy, Webern, and Schönberg required an "agonizing reappraisal" of traditional values. I shall mention only a few of the many contradictions implicit in this attitude. For example, though Messiaen admits that he is attracted to tonal ambiguity and polymodality, he still clings to the notion of a tonal axis, and insists on using, in one guise or another, the forms deriving from it. He occasionally indulges in *fugato* passages based on the outmoded principles of harmonic progression and symmetrical entries separated by intervals of a fifth. His examination of what might be retained of the sonata form led him to conclude that "there is only one aspect of that form which is obsolete: the recapitulation." Now it is the principle of recapitulation that has made the bithematic allegro the archetypal structure of classical music; no more forceful assertion of the tonal principle was ever devised, and it is worth noting that its decline coincided with the gradual disruption of form.[4] A composer who has come to realize that this basic element is "obsolete," and yet at the same time tries to reinstate certain concomitant elements (such as the terminal development), is merely endorsing the creation of a bastard form, derived from a

---

[4] Curiously enough, this error of Messiaen's is perfectly symmetrical to one Webern made in retaining the principle of recapitulation in a non-tonal context which ought normally to have precluded the very idea of such a thing.

conception which might be described as "infra-tonal." It also seems rather irresponsible to think that it is possible to solve the gigantic formal problems facing contemporary composers by borrowing a structure as elementary as the Gregorian Kyrie or by pouring into a single mold the ornate chorale arabesques of Bach, the style of the Hindu Ragas, and the patterns of the medieval sequences.

Now, since the basic component of music is no longer melody, harmony, or rhythm but *form*, no matter how skilfully Messiaen may transcribe, transform, and interpret bird calls, no matter how freely he may allow his "secret desire for enchantingly sumptuous harmony" to draw him, as he puts it, "toward those fiery swords, those sudden stars, those flows of blue-orange lava, those turquoise planets, the garnet-red and violet hues of those fibrous arborescences, those sounds and colors whirling in a rainbow jumble . . . ,"[5] no matter how much he may delight in simple rhythmic effects such as a special kind of "falling off" which he describes as "extremely graceful and refined" in its "tender nonchalance," his music is powerless to rise above the level of anecdote and the immediate intoxication of the senses. How can a composer of his caliber fail to realize that music demands more than this? Messiaen has proved capable of inventing only the most cursory formal order; he is probably the first to have realized its inadequacy, but with the result that he has turned to *disorder* for his salvation. After the compartmentalized works of his first period, whose effusive lyricism—inspired by the most dubious examples (one is reminded of Massenet, Tchaikovsky, and even, at times, of Gershwin)—hardly conceals their undeniably stilted form, after the almost pedantically austere works of his second, row-influenced

---

[5] This sentence, (taken from *Technique de mon Langage Musical*) ends as follows: "such a seething mass of chords must necessarily be philtered; only the sacred instinct of true, natural harmony is capable of doing this." Students of psychoanalysis will, I expect, take note of the way Messiaen spells "filtered."

period, it is not surprising that he should now have found his salvation in the seemingly hopeless "jumble" (to use one of his favorite words) of his recent works, based on the stylized use of bird calls.

For, in his late forties, Messiaen chose to enter into a kind of monastic retirement, far from the main streams of both classical and contemporary music. He himself has set forth the reasons for this decision in a rather disconcerting article: "In my hours of gloom, when I am suddenly aware of my own futility, when every musical idiom—classical, oriental, ancient, modern, and ultra-modern—appears to me as no more than admirable, painstaking experimentation without any ultimate justification, what is left for me but to seek out the true, lost face of music somewhere off in the forest, in the fields, in the mountains or on the seashore, among the birds. That is where music dwells for me, free, anonymous improvisations, sung for the sheer pleasure of singing, to greet the morning sun, charm the beloved, . . . sooth a tired body, or bid farewell to a bit of life as evening falls."[6]

Le Catalogue d'Oiseaux, because of its "endlessness"—the composer intends to work on nothing else until his death—is Messiaen's most characteristic work. Here the birds are set in their natural surroundings in the company of their neighboring denizens, and "everything is real: the melodies and rhythms of the solo birds, the counterpoint supplied by the melodies and rhythms of their neighbors, the answering calls, the medleys, the stretches of silence, and the relation between the calls and the time of day." In this work the composer has carried his highly literary conception of music to its utmost extreme. Messiaen's integrity and his respectful, analytical attitude toward works of music have somehow led him, through devious channels, "back to nature." Rejecting, it seems, even the musical legacy of his ancestors, Messiaen has returned to a form of pristine ex-

---

[6] In *Le Guide du Concert,* April 3, 1959.

pression, evolving a music which not only does not communicate through form but can dispense with it altogether; today's sophisticated sensibility relegates this sort of thing to the jukebox.

The very fact that he conceives of form in terms of "rules" automatically prevents Messiaen from inventing the new forms which would have enlivened his music. Taking refuge in a deliberately humble and necessarily precarious description of nature is merely a further compromise which, by a fitting irony of fate, has led him smack up against those very same obstacles he probably thought to avoid. Each piece in *Le Catalogue d' Oiseaux* is burdened with the very same shortcomings to be found in each of the *Vingt Regards*, and they stem from the same formal clichés (juxtaposition, compartmentalization, and the constant, periodic repetition of "love-themes"). The development of the musical tissue is determined by a descriptive program ("midnight: the music of the ponds and chorus of the frogs . . . six A.M.: sunrise, pink, orange, rose, mauve . . .") rather than by intrinsic structural requirements. I am afraid that the crushing word "futility" written by Messiaen himself, is applicable to this music, as well. Why can't the birds and their marvelous songs be left at peace in the forest?

I have not been able, in this short survey of Messiaen's music, to enter into its mystical implications. Am I really betraying the composer, however, by sticking to purely musical considerations? After all, as his disciple Yvonne Loriod reminds us, "Messiaen is a *musician!*" And he *is* a musician, one of noblest breed. It is strange that such a peerless *musician* should lack so many of the requisites of a *composer*. Messiaen has been called the successor of Debussy, but those who believe he is fail to realize that Debussy, in addition to his more obvious gifts, had a genius for *form* which we are only now beginning to understand. By dint of a tremendous and rigorous effort the composer of the *Cinq Rechants* could probably have salvaged a good many of his works. But if we are to believe the advice given future disciples in his treatise, Messiaen's conception of the composer's art is rather strange indeed. Just what is the meaning of these "favorite intervals," this "distorting prism of our musical language," this utilization of the melodic curves of the plainsong, permissible provided we "neglect their modes and rhythms in favor of our own"? What is the meaning of these "imitation folk songs" which are to be fabricated "without forgetting the little onomatopoeic refrain" and what, above all, does he mean by "taking a peek at other styles," allowing himself to "transform" a measure of Debussy—into a harmonic progression!—and using "the five notes which begin Mussorgsky's *Boris Godounov*" to concoct his "formula No. 1 for a melodic cadence" which he immediately provides with an "added time-value" and "harmonies from the second mode of limited transpositions"? Were these the methods of Mozart, Wagner, and Debussy, the composers whom Messiaen reveres above all and whose works he has so lovingly analyzed? One would like to think that this is merely a faulty pedagogical expression of a procedure which would otherwise be glaringly corrupt. Messiaen seems to be inviting his pupils to practice a technique of camouflage which might easily have been preached by a good many other so-called masters whom I can neither admire nor respect.

Camouflage and pupils; these two terms may well sum up Messiaen's career and define his role in musical history, for the one represents the most dubious and the other the most glorious side of his musical activities. The first makes him typical of his period and of that "doomed generation" of the twenties and thirties even though, despite his ultimate failure, he remains its most significant representative (insofar as his undeniable originality enabled him partly to transcend it). He expressed his generation's frightened reaction to the destruction of their language, but also perhaps the secret wish to take an active part in that destruction. He was the forerunner of a musical order which he rejects. At times, his love of the Orient brought him fairly close to "magical" poetic forces which, in some ways had already been harnessed by the greater genius of Igor Stravinsky. This, perhaps, was where his true path lay. Independently of its weaknesses, Messiaen's frozen music might perhaps have developed an incantatory fever which would have raised it to heights of relative grandeur. But his music is a voluptuous, ingrown world of subtle thrills, and lacks the essential spark of authentic violence. Deprived of this indispensable force, Messiaen's best pages, and even his most respectable achievement, *Les Trois Petites Liturgies*—an effeminate replica of *Les Noces*, though more static in its sensuous iridescence than Stravinsky's huge compact score—even his best pages lack that assertive power which is the sign of the authentic masterpiece.

If it is true, as Jean Barraqué has written, that his music, which has inspired no real disciples, "is the sole authority for the validity of the composer's aesthetic views," then the name of Olivier Messiaen is unlikely to be granted a place of honor in that great tradition which he felt he was keeping alive and helping to reform. I feel that he will go down in history as the teacher who, as Heinrich Strobel has so beautifully phrased it, "having thrown his grandiose imagination into the struggle against the insipid ideal of 'grace, form, and beauty' upheld by a certain kind of *musique française,* suddenly found himself supported by a few young people for whom music was not a trade, a social denomination, or a fashionable activity." It is through this second aspect of his career, his *pupils,* none of whom, save the very weakest, can actually be called his disciple, that posterity will remember the name of this great musician whose only crime was to be born during the most troubled period in history.

At the end of the last war, Messiaen's failure was not yet apparent, whereas that of twelve-tone row music, then still identified with the Vienna school, seemed complete. The specious elements in Schönberg's doctrine, the narrow, esoteric qualities of Webern's music prompted the least pessimistic observers to feel that the twelve-tone concepts had failed to live up to their promise; had, in fact, proven quite sterile. For the "school" founded by the three Viennese now offered nothing with which to challenge the apparent victory of the neo-classical reaction, nothing with which to counteract the influence of composers writing music crude enough to assimilate remnants of vernacular folk music, an easy road to comfortable, semi-official status. No worthwhile twelve-tone music was being written anywhere; a few plodding disciples dutifully perpetuated rules which already smacked of smug conformity, and that was all.

The only possible refuge for a spirit of true creation was in the generation then coming of age—a generation nurtured on the hardships of war and which now had to assert itself amidst the ruins of a broken world. Future historians, aided by their knowledge of works being conceived and written only now, will see those postwar years in their proper perspective; at present, however, the period appears to have been dominated by the unique experiment undertaken by a French composer. Once again, Paris took the lead in Europe's musical development. And yet the Parisian musical climate was hardly ripe for such a crucial adventure. Lulled into complacency by Debussy's worldwide reputation, the French were confident that the supremacy of their music had outlived the composer of *Pelleas*. Milhaud, Poulenc, and Sauguet were hailed as the new keystones of that traditional "light French touch" as against the "Germanic heaviness" of the Viennese school which was being rediscovered in France after twenty years of systematic neglect. Under these conditions, the teachings of Olivier Messiaen had both to revive traditional standards and impose new ones in order for Paris to stand out on the Western musical scene.

For while there is little doubt that Messiaen's was the only discipline in the world to have retained any vitality at all, the fact remains that his lessons would have been utterly useless had they not been poured into minds capable of transcending them. Messiaen's teachings combined an undivided love of great works with a strong aversion to all decadent forms of music and an infinite longing for fresh solutions; these qualities were of the sort capable of sparking in a young disciple's temperament the creative explosion that was so eagerly awaited. Reflective analysis was a form of intellectual exercise which might prepare a single mind for the immense task of embracing the world of music in *all* of its apparently irreconcilable aspects. Was there not some secret sign pointing to a possible future hidden beneath the debris of Western music waiting for someone to interpret it? Did not some of the prewar composers' ill-fated experiments contain the seeds of a successful venture still to be undertaken? Did not the music of the three great Viennese, of Stravinsky, Bartók, Messiaen, even that of Cage or Varèse, contain some secret spark that they themselves had failed to see?

A number of composers had already sensed that, on the other side of the mirror, so to speak, there existed a negative image of what had once been "musical beauty"; but none had been able to divine its outlines. Still, in abandoning tonality, music had entered into a singularly coherent universe of privative attributes. The new values were: rhythmic and melodic *dis*continuity, "*ir*rational" rhythm, "*a*thematicism," *non*-tonality, as well as the notion of constantly evolving forms. What no one knew as yet was that these were all potentially compatible.

> A composer of exceptional intellect was
> needed to hasten the return of a new, con-
> structive era. This historical challenge was
> met by a young man named Pierre Boulez.

CHAPTER SEVEN

Pierre Boulez

Boulez from 1944 to 1958

Pierre Boulez was born on March 26, 1925 in the little town of Montbrison in central France; his father was an industrialist. Boulez had originally intended to become a mathematician and studied for the entrance examination of the École Polytechnique. But he was also strongly attracted to music—he had sung in a choir as a child and dabbled in music at school—and after meeting Olivier Messiaen in Paris, he enrolled in 1944 in his harmony class at the Conservatory. In 1945 he was awarded a first prize in harmony. During the same period he studied counterpoint with Andrée Vaurabourg-Honegger and composition with Messiaen, who initiated him in the fine points of his own rhythmic idiom. That same year, Boulez tackled twelve-tone composition under the guidance of a musician of Polish origin, René Leibowitz. Boulez was immediately won over by the row system, the authentic modernity of which seemed immediately obvious to him. His first important works were: the Sonatine for flute and piano, the First Sonata for piano and, in a version for soloists, *Le Visage Nuptial;* all were written in 1946 and all were twelve-tone scores.

In 1946, Jean-Louis Barrault, who is not afraid of taking an occasional risk, appointed the twenty-one-year-old Boulez musical director of the troupe that he and Madeleine Renaud were organizing at the time. Thus relieved of the financial cares which had plagued the first years of his Paris venture, Boulez was able to devote most of his time to composition. The ten years spent with Barrault's company also gave him an opportunity to perfect his conducting technique (in the early stages of his career he received advice in this connection from that eminent technician, Roger Désormière). Boulez wrote only one piece of incidental theater music for Barrault, that which accompanied a production of Aeschylus' *The Oresteia* (1956).

First performed by Yvette Grimaud in the *Tryptique* concert series, Boulez's Second Piano Sonata (1947–1948) aroused violent controversy in *avant-garde* circles; the stinging articles in which he lashed out at his fellow composers in the most unconventional terms poured even more oil on the fire. The young man gave free reign to his aggressive temperament without the slightest heed for social decorum; even Messiaen, on the night of the first performance of his *Trois Talas*, was publicly accused of writing "bordello music." This incident alienated him from his former pupil for several years. Fired by the intransigence of youth, a small group of "Boulezistes" threw their weight behind the man who proclaimed Schönberg's doctrines a failure and was not afraid to reverse the order of importance generally used in assessing the three Viennese. Boulez's early supporters turned out to acclaim *Le Soleil des Eaux,* for solo voices and orchestra (1948) when fragments of it were first given by Désormière conducting the French National Orchestra. Although he was still practically unknown in France, his reputation began to grow in other countries, so swiftly in fact that during the fifties he came to be acknowledged as the leading international figure in twelve-tone music.

Le Livre pour Quatuor (1948–1949) and the second version of *Le Visage Nuptial,* for soloists, chorus, and full orchestra (1950–1951) were followed by a brief period during which this tireless worker seemed to slacken off. Actually, he was devoting his time to more frankly experimental compositions: *Polyphonie x,* for chamber orchestra (1951); two "music for tape" *Études,* done in the studios of the Research Group for Musique Concrète (1951–1952) and *Structures* for two pianos (begun in 1952). The first part of *Structures,* written as a tribute to Messiaen's *Mode de Valeurs et d'Intensités,* was first performed in 1952 as a part of the Festival de l'Oeuvre du Vingtième Siècle; it was played by Messiaen and Boulez, friendly again at last. In the midst of the performance, already punctuated by the cat-calls of listeners who were disconcerted by this esoteric music, a scandal broke out when a young "Bouleziste," the playwright Armand Gatti, at that time still an obscure reporter, took rather violent exception to the noisy protests of a woman who claimed to be a musician; the concert ended in utter confusion.

In 1954, under the auspices of the Renaud-Barrault Company, Boulez organized a series of concerts in the Petit Marigny Theater; the following year this series took the name of Domaine Musical. For the first concert, Barrault himself appeared in a pantomime performance of Stravinsky's *Renard,* conducted by Hermann Scherchen. Other eminent musicians subsequently took part in the concerts: the German pianists Alois Kontarsky and his brother Alphons, the American pianist David Tudor, the Italian flutist Severino Gazzeloni, the French pianist Yvonne Loriod, and the Austrian pianists Astrid and Hans-Otto Schmidt-Neuhaus; in 1957, Stravinsky came to Paris to direct *Agon* and in 1958 *Threni,* both as part of Domaine series. The great originality of these concerts, however, lay in the many first performances of works by young twelve-tone composers. Schönberg, Messiaen, Webern, and Varèse were paid due homage, but works by Karlheinz Stockhausen, Henri Pousseur, Luigi Nono, Michel Philippot, Michel Fano, and Earle Brown were also performed. Thanks to the Domaine, Paris once again assumed the prominent role in contemporary musical activities which it had gradually relinquished since the days of the Ballets Russes.

On June 18, 1955, the International Society for Contemporary Music, overriding the veto of its French delegation, sponsored the world première in Baden-Baden of *Le Marteau sans Maître* (1953–1954), conducted by Hans Rosbaud. Like *Le Soleil des Eaux* and *Le Visage Nuptial*, it was a setting of poems by René Char, but though longer than either of these earlier works, it was scored for only six instrumentalists and contralto. This is perhaps why it has received a good many public performances (in Paris, Vienna, Zurich, Munich, London, Aix-en-Provence, New York, and Los Angeles) as well as two commercial recordings (one conducted by the composer, the other by Robert Craft) and has become Boulez's best-known work.

Until then his reputation was more that of a theoretician and polemicist than a composer. His most important articles— "Eventuellement" (*La Revue Musicale*, April, 1952), "Auprès et au Loin" (*Cahiers de la Compagnie Renaud-Barrault*, 1954) and "Probabilités Critiques du Compositeur" (*Domaine Musical*, 1954) had earned him a reputation for "intellectualism" which zealous enemies took pains to spread. The name Boulez was on everyone's lips but his music was in very few ears. The success of *Le Marteau sans Maître* hastened his recognition as a composer and earlier works, previously considered impossible to play, received performances; in 1957, the Cologne Radio put on his most difficult score, *Le Visage Nuptial*, and the following year a revised version of *Le Soleil des Eaux* was performed at The Institute for Contemporary Music in Darmstadt. A Paris orchestra, the habitually conservative Association des Concerts Lamoureux, went so far as to commission a score for full orchestra, *Doubles*, composed in 1957 and first performed on March 16, 1958. Boulez played his Third Piano Sonata at its world première in September, 1957 at Darmstadt; both it and the first two *Improvisations sur Mallarmé*, for voice and various instruments, were composed that same year. Then, on October 19, 1958, the Donaueschingen festival (which, thanks to the clear-sighted friendship of Heinrich Strobel, had aided the young composer's career ever since 1951) organized the first performance of *Poésie pour Pouvoir* (1958), the first work in which Boulez mingled traditional instruments—divided into three orchestras—with the artificial sounds of "music for tape." It was now the turn of Boulez's renown as a composer to enhance his reputation as a writer; thenceforth his articles appeared in the major literary reviews ("Aléa" in *La Nouvelle Revue Française*, November, 1957).

Boulez's personality is diametrically opposed to Messiaen's on almost every count: he does not play the organ, he conducts; he does not teach, he organizes concerts; he does not write poetry but polemics; he is not a Catholic but an atheist. His speech is rapid and trenchant, his gestures sharp and precise; if by chance he is caught napping intellectually, he quickly counters with a new idea. Boulez the man is as brilliant as the composer; he likes to dominate and startle those who approach him, but he is also a charmer. Despite his gifts as a pianist, he remains a brilliant amateur (though his "presence" at the keyboard is worthy of the greatest virtuosos). He is a highly skilled conductor, and although he seems to have difficulty communicating with his men on the level of sensibility, he is possessed of a keen insight and a precise hand. In his writings he sometimes loses his temper to the point of insult and even vulgarity, but he is also capable of extremely rigorous dialectical analysis. Lastly, his musicianship is backed by an erudition and connoisseurship which until now has been lacking in all of his detractors. A reporter from *Time* magazine was a bit shocked when Boulez told him that Tchaikovsky was "abominable" and Brahms "a bore." These severe judgments are by no means irresponsible; he knows the merits of both these composers. To me, in fact, these opinions represent the most appealing side of Boulez's character, for they are merely the inevitable counterpart of any whole-hearted admiration for the truly great composers. Scores by Bach, Beethoven, and Debussy are surely the mainstays of a personal library, which must also contain the works of lesser stature with which this lucid, cultivated man is equally familiar.

The Early Works (*The Second Piano Sonata*)

When Boulez had finished his studies and parted with Messiaen and Leibowitz, the historical moment was such that a young composer, free to roam about in the jungle of contemporary music, needed a flawless lucidity. Many artists of our time intuitively feel the necessity to abolish consecrated forms; they sense the imminence of a new kind of poetic sensibility. But a fresh approach to musical poetics cannot be found overnight; it can stem only from the painstaking elaboration of a new language. By its very nature, music can exist only through its "morphology." Boulez felt that his most urgent task was an uncompromising reappraisal of music. It was not enough to write off tonal music in even more drastic terms than Schönberg had used; Boulez had to make a rigorous diagnosis of the present state of music as a whole. If there were positive elements to be found in the works written between the two World Wars—uneven, incomplete, and confused as they were—it was up to him to define and classify these elements. In other words, the construction of a new language presupposed an inventory of salvagable goods. All the elements that might conceivably be fitted together, all the trends that might possibly converge, had to be compared with an eye toward an ultimate symbiosis. The guiding principle of this association already existed in the twelve-tone row, but it had to be revised, enlarged and enriched.

Boulez's decision to accept complexity from the very outset was, I feel, one of his most important choices. The total assimilation of all the achievements of the great composers of the past, both recent and remote, had become an historical necessity, an imperative which could not be eluded. For having shirked this responsibility, a number of highly gifted composers were doomed to impotence from the very start. Their decision to ignore this or that major experiment was dictated less, perhaps, by their fear of losing contact with a public as ignorant as they in this respect, than by the fear that they would ultimately have to grapple with the subsequent developments of that formidable complexity. Though often their withdrawal into a spuriously simplified idiom was disguised by political or "social" motives, it was actually nothing more than a frightened reaction to the inextricable entanglements of the contemporary world. The very nature of Boulez's mind, on the contrary, steered him straight down the middle of this arduous path, and the difficulties encountered were, for him, a form of reward. At the same time, his down-to-earth realism saved him from the wild extremes to which other, less orderly thinkers were carried by similar reasoning.

Exacerbated lyricism and controlled violence were the main traits of the young composer who, at the age of twenty-two, undertook to write his Second Piano Sonata. This as yet little-known score holds a particularly significant, pivotal position in the works composed by Boulez between 1946 and 1950. One might say that his previous works built up to this sonata, while *Le Livre pour Quatuor* and the two vocal works with orchestra were commentaries on it. Poetically speaking, *Le Soleil des Eaux* and the revised version of *Le Visage Nuptial* were both steeped in the fury which drove the young composer, but the Second Sonata, in its most fiery passages, was the very incarnation of that fury. In this work, a great composer came into his own. The Sonata constituted a break with the aesthetics of Webern, both in style and dimensions. One feels that Boulez found the narrow limits of the Piano Variations too restrictive, and Webern's attempt to broaden them, which ultimately produced the two Cantatas, still far too timid; a bolder return to large-scale forms seemed necessary. Webern's splendid sensitivity, however, had enabled him to adjust the means to suit the end, so that an expansion of musical dimensions had to be accompanied by a basic transformation of style. This is where Boulez displayed his exceptional temperament, subjecting the rigorous but static lines of Webern's style to an incandescent blast, as it were. Thus, by the most devious paths, twelve-tone row music was finally brought face to face with that marvelous discovery, completely forgotten since Debussy, the improvisational style. The Second Sonata may be regarded as an attempt at improvisation within a structural framework of great complexity. Naturally, the work is imperfect. It reflects the successive discoveries, the leaps and pirouettes of a thought process in full effervescence; the final variations in the third movement, for example, are not of the same caliber as those that precede. And yet, for all its fitful counterpoint and the rough spots in its disjunct, sforzando-ridden phrasing, the Second Sonata offers a pianistic style as vigorous as Liszt's: well-balanced, coherent, and perfectly adapted to the instrument. This style, which completely renews the possibilities of the piano by combining Stravinsky's metallic percussiveness with a sense of sumptuous aural effect, leaves far behind it Bartok's monotonous poundings and Messiaen's redundant post-impressionism.

Just as the Romantic conception of keyboard music fostered a new piano technique, so Boulez has invented a whole set of movements—a new forearm position, a rigid sforzando attack, etc.—which constitute a fresh approach to piano playing and were immediately taken up and developed by virtuoso pianists like Yvonne Loriod and David Tudor. The style of writing and the variety of attacks obtained through this new method concur to give the piano a new sonority. This transformation, however, would be completely useless were it not allied to new musical conceptions. Boulez's primary contribution to music in the Second Piano Sonata consists of a new attitude towards the relationships between rhythm and melody. The *serial* organization of this work goes beyond the narrow limits of strict tone-row composition; whereas hitherto the rows were set forth in their entirety, here they are cut up in pieces, giving rise to a number of melodic cells composed of characteristic intervals and upon which the rhythmic cells have the effect of a chemical reagent. The rhythmic idiom proper, with its changing and interchanging of values, its transformations of *rational* (or binary) note-values into *irrational* note-values (triplets, quintuplets, etc.) and its contrapuntal superpositions of rhythms subjected to an indefinite number of variations, is highlighted in return by acute polyphonic combinations. This rigorous approach to rhythmic construction *within a complex framework* was completely new; but even more novel and more decisive was the great malleability afforded by these raw materials. The rhythmic idiom of the Second Sonata does not derive from the unhampered multiplications of a fundamental time-value, as did those of *Les Noces* or *Turangalîla*, but tends, on the contrary, to destroy such time-values by changes in the tempo and metric unity and by the extensive use of irrational time-values.

Aside from the negligible stylistic elements borrowed from Messiaen (these still crop up in the Third Sonata, written ten years later), Boulez's debt to his teacher, as well as the differences between the two composers, is fairly clear in this work. The regeneration and extension of tone-row music were not carried out by the pupils of Schönberg or Webern but by those of Messiaen, a fact which would seem to prove that the Frenchman's rhythmic discoveries were indeed fruitful. For although Messiaen's rhythmic architecture may seem weak and, if the truth be told, outdated, it did, in some ways, foreshadow Boulez's "compound structures." Then, too, though Messiaen never felt the urgent need for a concept of "irrational rhythms," he was able to convey to his erstwhile disciples his "sense of rhythmic unrest"; in so doing, he was inevitably preparing the day when he would be by-passed by others, but he enabled Boulez to introduce the malleability afforded by irrational rhythm into his music at a very early stage, which may be regarded as a truly emancipating step.

The Laboratory Years

The last devotees of Schönberg maintain that the composer of *Pierrot Lunaire* made all the major intuitive discoveries of his period. Similarly, it may one day be possible to say that Boulez "thought of everything" as well; insofar as he shares this opinion, he is not averse to having thought of "everything" first. For this composer's exceptional mind is essentially that of an experimenter; in this sense, he may be regarded as the archetypical artist of our experimental century. He seldom considers a score to have reached its definite state. It is not unusual for him to rework music which seemed completely finished, transforming a suite of incidental music into a cantata (*Le Soleil des Eaux*) or a chamber work into a fresco for orchestra and chorus (*Le Visage Nuptial*), adding new pieces to an already established set (*Structures, Le Marteau sans Maître*) or, like Joyce, acquainting the public with fragments of a "work in progress" (Third Piano Sonata). The Second Piano Sonata is one of a series of works involving experiments in every possible domain. In *Le Visage Nuptial*, he incorporated quarter tones into the row, and in the orchestral version of this same score experimented with a minutely partitioned string section (sixteen different parts for the first violins); in *Le Soleil des Eaux*, he established an absolute discontinuity between speaking, chanting, and singing in the vocal parts which produced a kind of verbal disintegration, while in *Le Livre pour Quatuor* he experimented with highly differentiated intensities. This pivotal score, while it still contains echos of the Second Sonata, was also the first in which Boulez displayed the concern for problems of organization which was to dominate his next two works, *Polyphonie x* and *Structures*.

Up to this point in his career, Boulez's work had illustrated various stages in the conquest of a virgin soil, a conquest founded on the elaboration of a new language. Boulez the composer does not balk at turning theoretician, and likes to be able to justify each new attainment in terms of the great music of the past. His famous analysis of *The Rite of Spring* was more than an attempt to elucidate Stravinsky's music; he was looking for historical examples on which to ground his own dissociation of rhythm and melody; he discovered the remote origins of his procedure in the isorhythmic motets of Philippe de Vitry, Guillaume de Machaut, and Guillaume Dufay. "Thus," writes Boulez, "though today many music lovers and even composers may find it very hard to believe, it is clear that rhythmic structures could exist prior to the writing of the actual notes. . . . Rhythm must first be delivered of that so-called spontaneity which has generally been ascribed to it for so long; delivered, that is, of its condition as the literal expression of polyphony and promoted to the rank of primordial structural factor by acknowledging the possibility of its pre-existence to polyphony; all of which will ultimately establish even tighter and far more subtle bonds between rhythm and polyphony."[1] Boulez's attitude in *Polyphonie x* was purely experimental and his goal a single system which would co-ordinate all the components of music: height, depth, and duration of the notes, tone-color, types of attacks, registers and intensities, all were to be controlled, if not actually determined, by the serial principle. This project was, of course, over-ambitious; one cannot possibly hope to achieve the "cosmic" organization of a universe which is not even fully explored as yet. Compared with *The Art of the Fugue*, which constituted the end-result of

---

[1] Pierre Boulez: "Stravinsky Demeure," in *Musique Russe* (I), pp. 223–224.

hundreds of years of experience in contrapuntal imitation, *Polyphonie x* is no more than a courageous exercise, a further step toward the reconquest of stylistic rigor; it still "falls short of aural realities" and is sometimes rather hard for the listener to take. (This is why Boulez will not allow it to be performed in its present state.)

In his experimental works Boulez completed his reconstruction of polyphony through a new musical grammar. They contain a great many technical inventions: "magic squares" which serve to interlock several tone-rows and set up correspondences between notes and time-values; tone-color structures; combinations of attacks and intensities which may or may not be linked with polyphonic structures; "positive and negative images" of a given rhythm, in which sound and silence change places; extensions of Webern's dialectic of registers, etc. As one may imagine, all these notions will be a part of future treatises on composition, but Boulez quite rightly protests that he is more than a mere grammarian. His stinging epithets lampoon those for whom composition is, in the last analysis, nothing but "a conditioned reflex," "a careful form of bookkeeping." "When composition," he says, "takes the form of a distributive economy, no matter how elegant or ingenious, it is doomed to futility and pointlessness." His cruel jibes do not spare the out-of-date exponents of Schönberg's twelve-tone theories ("juggling numbers at high speed is not enough to constitute an insurance policy on genius"), any more than the smug admirers of French "lucidity and elegance" ("they love to mix Descartes with high-fashion dress-designing"). His attempt to restore the composer's sense of integrity, degraded by predecessors who "had no higher ambition than those of the bricklayer or whore," has led him to an exalted conception of human genius: *"There is no true creation except in the unforeseeable's becoming necessity."*[2] Yet he is by no means contemptuous of grammar, is

---

[2] Pierre Boulez: "Eventuellement."

aware of its importance, but insists upon its subordination to poetics.

It would be very shortsighted of me to reduce Boulez's music to a set of technical inventions. Over and above their purely syntactical significance, these inventions are part of an undertaking of larger scope: the expansion of the formal universe foretokened in the music of Webern. By carrying the "serial" notion beyond its original goal—beyond, that is, the organization of the twelve-tone scale—by extending it to all the other components of music, Boulez performed an act of tremendous but still largely unforeseeable consequences. In this light, the disrepute into which the terms "twelve-tone row" and "dodecaphonic" have fallen is highly significant, for the word "series" has come to signify the *delimitation of a network of possibilities,* a texturization of aural space. The first results of this forward stride have been felt on the level of form. Debussy had already implicitly rejected the notion of the preconceived form, preferring that his music invent itself as it went along. Similarly, Boulez does not hesitate to apply to music Sartre's aphorism, "existence precedes essence." But he is in a position to put this formal freedom—now bounded only by the limits of the serial network of possibilities—to more active use, since no tonal or thematic functions exist to interfere with the work's successive transformations. Henceforth, a *serial world,* basically different from the *tonal world* defined by the great works of the classical repertory, has become a reality.

The Sound-Object

After the climactic experiment carried out in *Polyphonie x*—the bold, uncompromising purity of which is, in one sense, quite admirable—technical problems gradually took a back seat in Boulez's creative activities. He felt himself drawn to experiments with new areas of music; he also became more concerned with having his works performed in public. Without losing sight of his experimental vocation, he began setting himself limited goals and no longer allowed the joys of experimentation to take precedence over the concrete realities of performance. *Structures,* though a further attempt to institute a total serial organization, nevertheless constituted a "return to the concert-hall"; by using only two pianos instead of the eighteen instruments required by *Polyphonie x,* he deliberately avoided one of the major difficulties of such an enterprise. More recent works, such as *Le Marteau sans Maître* and *Improvisations sur Mallarmé* contained no experimental efforts whatsoever, but were merely further applications of his past discoveries. Gradually, a sense of caution pervaded Boulez's music.

Boulez was no doubt still primarily concerned with innovation, but began pursuing this goal with different tools and in a different domain. An artist's career often takes these impalpable turnings. The intellectual climate evolves, he is obsessed by new ideas, certain goals have lost their meaning, others are found to be out of reach and are abandoned. The old incentives are replaced by new ones which may reflect an *unforeseeable necessity* of a strictly personal order; they may also betoken the artist's realization that the poetic universe which, in his youthful enthusiasm, had seemed to him infinite is, in fact, all too circumscribed; this discovery may well result in a series of works, extending from a *Mavra* to a *Rake's Progress,* in which the composer seeks to repudiate his *Rite of Spring.*

Three main features, I feel, define Boulez's recent work. The first is a concern with *polished style* which has been a constant factor in his work ever since *Le Marteau sans Maître.* The second is his attempt to achieve ever-evolving forms; this was already implicit in his early works but has been made explicit in the Third Sonata by the incorporation of a new parameter into his music, that of *chance.* Lastly, in his two *Études* and in *Poésie pour Pouvoir,* he has sought to diversify musical space by peopling it with "sound-objects" capable of being handled serially, and by incorporating the stereophonic dimension into this spatial organization.

By its very nature, this last-named project was closely related to the experiments of 1951 and 1952, and was first expressed in two short pieces (entitled *Étude I* and *Étude II*) conceived and executed while he was taking the laboratory course given for Paris composers by Pierre Schaeffer and his *Groupe de Musique Concrète:* it constitutes a response to the experiments of Edgar Varèse and John Cage, in which Boulez has often displayed considerable interest.

These two Americans[3] are the most famous representatives of New York's musical *avant-garde,* and though their works are outwardly very different, they do share the same basic aim: both wish to reappraise the raw material of sound and make it a primary factor in music. Debussy had consecrated the power of sound *per se;* Varèse has tried to elaborate a music in which the headiness of sheer aural sensation would attain such a degree of incantory violence as to dispense with rhetoric altogether. Cage has attempted to carry even farther the listener's impression of other-worldliness through the use of homemade "sound-objects" which no longer bear any relationship to the usual instrumental tone-colors and do away with the division of the octave into twelve equal half tones. As both men wished their music to be neither tonal, modal, nor dodecaphonic, rhythm was the only principle upon which they could possibly develop it. Although they were, in this respect, precursors of Boulez, their work displays no signs of any remarkable rhythmic gifts, and if its very conception seems rather feeble today, the fault lies with the flagrant inadequacy of their respective idioms. For while the unleashed fury of the thirteen percussion groups used in *Ionisation* and the savage shrieks of the wind instruments in *Intégrales* brought to the attention of composers everywhere the strange

---

[3] Edgar Varèse is of French descent; he was born in Paris on December 22, 1885 and moved to the United States in 1916. John Cage was born in Los Angeles on September 15, 1912.

works of Edgar Varèse, which seemed to show that music might exist independently of any harmonic, contrapuntal, or even melodic considerations, and although John Cage's *prepared piano*[4] is not universally regarded as a quaint gag-machine, "a percussion-piano the soundboard of which seems overgrown with some sort of queer, metallic vegetation,"[5] the fact remains that no major composer has followed in the footsteps of these two independent artists.

The attitudes of both Varèse and Cage are diametrically opposed to that of Boulez in one very important respect, for while the composer of *Le Soleil des Eaux* fully assumes the legacy of his predecessors, from Debussy to Messiaen, it is as though the two New Yorkers wished their experiments to remain completely apart from any tradition whatsoever; like the surrealists, they probably feel that this attitude is an assertion of what they take for absolute creative freedom. This total rejection of the past has led them to experiment with a wide variety of solutions, such as those involving improvisation (Cage was probably the first composer to have consciously made a place for chance in his music). In other respects, their paths have often been widely divergent. Toward the end of his career, for example, Varèse has been attracted to "music for tape"—a logical extension of his conceptions—and in 1954 presented a large-scale work called *Deserts* to a Parisian audience which gave it a painfully memorable reception; the performance of this work involved a combination of pre-recorded material with music played on ordinary instruments in the concert hall. During that same period, Cage and David Tudor gave recitals on two prepared pianos in which

---

[4] To "prepare" a piano, one slips various wooden or metal objects between the strings; their presence considerably alters the tone-color of certain notes and even, at times, transforms them into "complex sounds" of indeterminate pitch.

[5] Pierre Boulez: "Eventuellement." This partial quotation may give the impression that Boulez is making fun of Cage; as it happens, this is not the case.

the sound-objects, often handled humorously, were juxtaposed or superposed, irrespective of any tempo, explicit or implicit—duration and frequency being regulated by that least musical of all instruments, the stop watch.

As one might imagine, Boulez's keen intellect did not fail to see how un-rigorous and aesthetically unsuccessful these experiments were; nevertheless, he was able to profit by them. For though he is the most recent "organizer" of the twelve-tone system, he has always kept one eye on the development of techniques aimed at transcending the total chromatic. In *Le Visage Nuptial,* he had made an effort to incorporate quarter tones into serial polyphony, and had soon been attracted to the complex sounds of *musique concrète*.[6] The founder of this "movement," Pierre Schaeffer, is a dilettante with a bent for the wildest ventures, and had at first looked upon sound-objects as the makings

---

[6] Composers of *musique concrète* begin by recording various sounds (either musical sounds or noises of indeterminate pitch) and then, by speeding them up, slowing them down, filtering or inverting them, metamorphose these sounds into "sound-objects" (*objets sonores*) whose origin it is not always possible to distinguish. This technique is still rather precarious, and allows for a degree of approximation that prevents the authentic composer from writing out his score before selecting the raw material, which is often impossible to transcribe. By splicing together the magnetic tapes containing the material to be manipulated, the composer reconstitutes his work and enables it to be communicated to listeners. *Electronic music*, on the other hand (not to be confused with electronic instruments such as the Ondes Martenot or the Theremin), uses *purely musical* sounds of electronic origin which may, eventually, be transformed as well. Electronic techniques are more accurate, making it possible to compose a work on paper, and they lend themselves admirably to a serial organization of non-tempered musical space. It would seem, however, that electronic sounds do not yet have the same quality of "other-worldliness" found in certain sound-objects produced by *musique concrète*. But then, these two techniques are by no means incompatible, and it is likely that the future development of music for tape will require that composers make indiscriminate use of all electrophonic techniques, as did Boulez in *Poésie pour Pouvoir*.

of strange, poetic sound-effects and nothing more. Later, he rather ingenuously conceived the idea of arranging them in various patterns, much like visible objects; this was a somewhat tardy equivalent of the permutation methods used by the first twelve-tone composers. It was Boulez who first brought an attitude of implacable discipline to *musique concrète*, subject until then to the whims of amateurs. His *Études* were as wholly experimental as *Polyphonie x*, and contained a number of contributions which gave real meaning to the notion of "music for tape." For example, Boulez was not afraid to divide up sound-

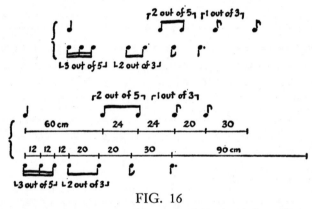

FIG. 16

Graph showing how incomplete groups of irrational time-values can be obtained by editing two synchronized tapes together.

objects according to the serial concept, thereby creating a microcosm that was set vibrating, as it were, by various inversions and permutations. A new continuity was then obtained by cutting and resplicing the magnetic tape. Editing techniques also afford the composer an unprecedented freedom in the handling of rhythm. Many irrational rhythmic structures which simply cannot be played by any orchestra and still others, even more complex, which are beyond the grasp of the most accomplished soloist, can be easily elaborated and heard in all their perfection thanks to precise editing (Fig. 16).

The significance of these two experimental pieces overshadows their undeniable failure as works of art, for they provide dignified proof that musical materials of a non-dodecaphonic nature are capable of being organized along serial lines. Though they sprang from two different levels of human sensibility, the serial concept and the sound-object realize their secret affinities. One is tempted to interpret this as the gradual disclosure of an order already virtually existent. Was it mere coincidence that electrophonic techniques of sound production emerged at the same time that a related phenomenon, the sound-object, made its first appearance under various guises in the instrumental works of Webern, Varèse, and Cage? Was it merely an accident that the possibilities afforded by tape-recording and editing were revealed at a time when rhythmic complexity threatened to confound human physical capacities, opening a breach between composer and performer? Was it not strange that composers should have begun to feel that they might one day exhaust the possibilities of the orchestra at the very moment when techniques were invented enabling them to transcend the orchestra?

Stereophonic Music

And yet the orchestra is still struggling to survive. To do so, it must adapt itself to the requirements of the new music, it must, in particular, provide an adequate reply to the latest challenge in music—one which may fast become tyrannical—the stereophonic effect.

I am not yet sure I understand the exact significance of the sudden appearance of stereophony in music, but I do know that it may well have revolutionary consequences, that it may finish reshuffling the hierarchical setups inherited from the past. Mozart's melodic gift now seems to us his basic trait; the time may come when the most striking sign of a composer's genius may be his flair for stereophonic effect. This is not as unlikely as one might think, since a number of composers have already been fascinated by this strange world. They see stereophonic sound as more than a souped-up form of high fidelity, more than a Hollywood bonus for wide-screen movie fans; for them, it represents a new dimension added to the auditory compass, one capable of setting up new types of structures. By taking into account a new co-ordinate, *the directional source of sound*, composers can add an *acoustical dimension* to the existing *musical dimension*, which is defined by the co-ordinates *note* and *tone-color*. This idea was latent in the works of certain old masters, but medieval antiphony (and its later, more sumptuous developments, such as the double choirs at Saint Mark's in Venice or the choral frescos in *The Saint Matthew Passion*) involved a simple alternation, a contrasting relief; modern stereophony combines the direction and the intensity of sound in a symbiosis which the "athematic" character of the sound-object renders surprisingly malleable.

In his *Études*, Boulez was more concerned with serial problems than with stereophonic ones, and these two pieces employ only a kind of *static* stereophonic relief, involving three sound-sources. But *kinematically*, stereophonic sound does already exist: the sound-object hardly allows the listener time to identify it before it is revolving around him, rising and falling in space. "Electronic" composers working in Cologne (Eimert and Stockhausen) and in Milan (Maderna and Berio) have developed the possibilities of this exciting technique, and at the Brussels World's Fair of 1958, Varèse was able to take advantage of special technical installations[7] placed at his disposal by a large manufacturer of electronic equipment. Therefore, when Boulez again turned his attention to music for tape after a lapse of several years, the stereophonic field had already been extensively prospected.

In any case, he had not lost sight of the problem during the interval. Taking his cue from Stockhausen, he had carried it

_____

[7] Over four hundred sources of sound, co-ordinated by cybernetic relays.

over into the orchestra, and for the world-première of *Doubles* called for changes in the usual arrangement of the orchestra. "I feel I may assert," he wrote "without fear of contradiction, that when different tone-colors are played in rapid succession they ought not to have to cling desperately to one another across an obstacle of distance; nor will I be contradicted if I say that the modern ear requires clarity and motion, and therefore feels a need of stereophonic effect. This 'manifestation' achieved by a new arrangement of the instruments of the orchestra is actually required by the new music's written texture, ultimately, therefore, by its poetic essence." *Doubles* was written for a conventional symphony orchestra; the reform attempted in this work involved the arrangement of the instruments on the stage. Instead of being grouped in the customary sections, they were arranged in a pattern that took into account the work's structural necessities. Thus Boulez was attempting to duplicate, within the orchestral framework—and on a smaller scale of course—the conditions for *kinematic stereophony*, previously possible only through the techniques of music for tape. The unreliable acoustics of the Salle Pleyel were hardly suited to an attempt of this sort, and the experiment remained inconclusive. Still, it represented an effort to revise orchestral concepts which should one day bear real fruit.

In a larger work performed the following autumn (1958), at the Donaueschingen festival—*Poesie pour Pouvoir* based on a text by Henri Michaux—Boulez employed three instrumental groups—soloists, brass, and strings with woodwinds—placed under the joint direction of two conductors. Like Varèse's *Deserts*, it also makes use of pre-recorded electrophonic elements. One wonders whether this difficult marriage of the orchestra and music for tape is not instrumental music's last hope of survival before the orchestra finally becomes a kind of museum, with the sole permanent function of perpetuating the classical masterpieces. The creative activities of our chief composers, however, prove that they are well aware of this danger, and their daring orchestral conceptions allow one to feel that that day is still a long way off. It is not yet assured that the need for stereophonic effect will ultimately do away with the orchestra altogether, but the orchestra will probably have to undergo extensive transformations because of it.

Chance Makes Its Appearance

The work of Pierre Boulez occupies a central position in contemporary music and may be described as a compendium of today's most characteristic experiments and goals. It is not surprising, therefore, that the scope of his influence grew so rapidly that by the time he was thirty he was the undisputed head of a new school of composers. His experience was too significant not to be emulated, and though his conceptions have had little effect on twelve-tone composers of the previous generation—Křenek, Dallapiccola, Frank Martin, André Souris, Milton Babbitt—they have greatly influenced the work of postwar composers. The Frenchmen Michel Philippot, Michel Fano, Maurice Le Roux, Gilbert Amy, and Michel Ciry; the Italians Luigi Nono, Bruno Maderna, and Luciano Berio; the Belgian Henri Pousseur; and the Swede Bo Nilsson, among many others, have all been influenced by Boulez's notions but with different degrees of success.[8] So far, however, the latter has encountered only one serious rival as an innovator: the German composer Karlheinz Stockhausen.[9]

With very few exceptions, these young composers seem not to have succeeded in overcoming the contradictions to which

---

[8] Independently of any technical affinities, it hardly seems necessary to emphasize the enormous difference between a piece of hack-work signed Alexander Goehr or André Boucouretchliev and a work as lively and colorful as Pousseur's *Mobile,* an undeniably successful piece of piano-writing.

[9] Karlheinz Stockhausen was born in Altenberg (a town near Cologne) in 1928. He studied with Frank Martin, then with Messiaen; he has specialized partly in experimental electronic music.

they are exposed by virtue of their historical situation. The influence of Webern on this group is still strong, inhibiting their attempt to overtake Boulez in his daring speculations. Yet all are fascinated by his conceptions; the man and his theories convey a sort of intellectual intoxication, accompanied by a musical "one-upmanship" which sometimes proves rather dangerous. Thus, the discovery of irrational rhythmics has been utilized by certain composers of the new generation without the slightest concern for practical considerations. In the past ten years more music has been written than ever before which it is impossible to play—or only so approximately as to make a mockery of the works' apparent rigor. Stockhausen, in his first *Klavierstücke*, was not the least impulsive of these experts in complication. Today this young composer, whose *Gesang der Jünglinge* is the most famous piece of "electronic" music to date, implicitly acknowledges the fact that one cannot push subtlety in instrumental rhythm quite so far. His subsequent works have contained other, more far-reaching ideas which in turn have influenced Boulez. Stockhausen is one of those composers who has endowed stereophony with a true musical content, first in his music for tape and later in his experiment with a triple orchestra. After undergoing the influence of Webern's somewhat rigid row conceptions in his early orchestral works—such as *Kontrapunkte*—and after devoting himself to the composition of works "for tape," gigantic "sound-objects in time" which completely excluded the notion of interpretive performance, he felt the need for a new kind of freedom (just as did Boulez, after *Polyphonie x* and *Structures*). In his *Zeitmasse* for woodwind quintet, he introduced the notion of "controlled chance" into certain cadenza-like passages by deliberately allowing the performers a certain interpretive freedom.

With his *Klavierstücke XI*, composed a few months later in 1956, Stockhausen took a leap into the unknown; this work breaks with a convention accepted by every composer since the Renaissance, that of the *unicity* of the written work. The piece was given its world première in New York on April 22, 1957 by David Tudor, who played it twice through during the same concert; every person present in the Carl Fischer Concert Hall was aware that even the length of the piece differed considerably from one performance to the other. The score is printed on a single, unusually large sheet of paper the size of an architect's blueprint. It comprises nineteen short, separate episodes which the performer may play in any order he sees fit; the work comes to an end when any given episode has been repeated twice. The composer has devised conventions governing the succession of tempos and intensities, with the result that a given section may, according to the itinerary "chosen" by the performer, change character completely each time it is played. As one can see, this conception allows the work to assume hundreds of contrasting shapes without affecting its essence. In contrast with the solid, definitive quality of electronic music, Stockhausen has created an absolutely fluid work which cannot possibly be captured by any recording. The pianist does not, however, *improvise;* he merely brings into play the factor of *chance,* thereby promoting it to the supreme role of a determinant factor in musical form. A work conceived along these lines no longer determines its own path, as in Debussy's conception, but lends itself instead to an infinite number of virtual developments, all of them equally possible. As it was immediately remarked at the time, a parallel may be drawn between this conception and that of Calder's mobiles.

With *Le Marteau sans Maître,* Boulez had just abandoned the austere limits of strict form to which he had deliberately confined himself until then. In his articles of that period he was setting forth the principles of a new "rigorous style," but was also vaunting the possibilities of a "free style." His notions on form led him to seek an axis which would intercept both poles. One may well imagine the fresh incentive he derived from the sudden appearance of chance in musical composition. But though Boulez was undoubtedly attracted to the new and unexpected possibilities afforded by Stockhausen's invention, several reservations prevented his adhering to it wholeheartedly. The most disturbing aspect of the German composer's variation-system was that it seemed to postulate that "any rhythmic structure may be organically adapted to any tempo"; Boulez rejected this notion. Similarly, the Frenchman could not accept Stockhausen's unlimited cycle of permutations. He too wished to endow the musical work with an "open cycle of possibilities" in contradiction with the classical conception, but he insisted upon maintaining the notion of composition (which Stockhausen's approach may, in some respects, be said to abolish).

Boulez's Third Piano Sonata—which he calls a "book" or "work in progress"—takes Stockhausen's invention into account, but involves a reappraisal of its basic elements. This sonata is a dazzling work, the piano style of which, though oddly reminiscent of Messiaen's, constitutes an effort to draw new effects of resonance from the instrument. When first performed, it comprised five pieces—1. *Antiphonie;* 2. *Trope;* 3. *Constellation;* 4. *Strophe;* 5. *Séquence*—which Boulez calls "formatives" (*formants* in French) which should later give rise to "developments" by interaction. *Antiphonie* and *Séquence* on the one hand, and *Trope* and *Strophe* on the other, form two pairs of pieces which may be arranged in any symmetrical order around the central and longest piece, *Constellation*. Each piece allows for possibilities of choice, but these are carefully codified. The pianist may invert or omit whole passages, choose between two alternative circuits, switch from one circuit to another at given points or even transpose entire structures (this by means of "magic squares" and tablatures which have not yet been entirely worked out). The range of possible itineraries is quite wide, but infinitely less so than in the *Klavierstücke XI*. The role of chance is therefore proportionally reduced, so that one may, indeed, speak of *controlled freedom* in connection with this work.[10]

Form and Style (Le Marteau sans Maître)

In contrast with the zig-zag course deliberately steered by Stockhausen, Boulez established an "undetermined itinerary which is a function of time—a given number of problematic events being fitted into an elastic duration—but which nevertheless develops according to a logical pattern and with an overall sense of direction, an itinerary which may include caesura in the form of pauses or 'sound platforms,' and which moves distinctly from a beginning to an end."[11] It is interesting to note that the composer of the Third Sonata feels that he has thus "respected the notion of finish and the closed cycle of the Western musical work," while at the same time "introducing the element of chance and the open structure of Eastern works."

By refusing the final stroke of daring which would have rid form completely of the one element of constraint inherent in all composed music, that of *pre-existence*—a composition *exists* prior to its performance—Boulez, though he is open to any idea which might contribute to the elaboration of a "relative

---

[10] It is conceivable that despite this salutary prudence—or perhaps because of it—Boulez' influence on young musicians may be on the wane. Instead of taking the trouble to ponder over the exact significance of Stockhausen's spectacular challenge, they preferred simply to go him one better, adding a dash of their own ingenuity—or extravagance, as the case may be. Thus Stockhausen is tending to become the leader of a movement whose principal members are the Argentinean Mauricio Kagel and the Italian Sylvano Bussoti, as well as a few newcomers, most of them Germans, who have studied at the Darmstadt seminary. It is well for even the most dubious experiments to be carried out sincerely. The future will tell whether this is merely a vogue, or whether the forms born of chance's encounter with set structures will be able to exorcise the threat of compartmentalization which hangs over them already.

[11] Pierre Boulez: "Aléa," in *La Nouvelle Revue Française*, November, 1957.

formal virtuality," nevertheless condemns those which tempt the composer to elude "the choice inherent in all forms of creation." Reoriented in this way, Stockhausen's idea provides an opportunity to "absorb chance," transforming it into an additional tool for destroying immanent structures. As Boulez writes: "The adaptation of the serial concept to composition itself . . . by incorporating the more general notion of permutation into structural organization—a permutation the limits of which are rigorously defined in terms of the restrictions placed on its powers by the very fact of its self-determination—constitutes a logical and fully justified development, since both 'morphology' and rhetoric are governed by one and the same principle of organization."[12] Serial permutation, which constitutes a microcosmic factor in the work, also becomes a formal principle, thereby acting upon a macrocosmic level. This notion is a remarkable extension of the system elaborated by Boulez ten years earlier; it represents a fresh attempt to elaborate that absolutely modern form which would seem to be the ultimate goal of each of his creative acts, a goal which he might well have reached were it not for the fact that this form can, in the last analysis, stem only from the constant readaptation of a system to the requirement of each new work. Even the Second Sonata was more daring in its structural details than in its overall form, since its four movements still owed a certain allegiance to classical patterns. Though alive with fire, it did not achieve that ultimate grandeur of absolute uniqueness.

Doing away with the remains of the archetypal forms that constituted the basis of the classical masterpieces is only half the battle, in any case; greater challenges are still to be met. Can the contemporary work as such live in its own, fully assumed freedom, independently of any and every formal tie? Can it lay claim to its own *incomparable* destiny and display complete originality even in its most secret essence? This is the awe-

---

[12] *Ibid.*, p. 854.

inspiring vision which seems to have been—still is, perhaps—the goal of Pierre Boulez. He may well be trying to "isolate" an unclassifiable work which somehow slips through his fingers with each new score. The Third Sonata offers intelligent solutions to the problems raised by the incorporation of chance into music, but one wishes that the work itself made the necessity of these solutions *existentially* apparent on a poetic level.

The same holds true for the second *Improvisation sur Mallarmé;* true, its utter dislocation of rhythm does further develop the notion of "fluctuating time" by replacing the relatively strict meter of tonal music with an irregular beat (the conductor sometimes directs with conventional signs, while the singer may have to articulate in a single breath and according to her possibilities a phrase composed solely of organ-points—cf. Fig. 17), but on an aesthetic level the work does not make as much of this new development as one might have hoped. And though I grant that this may merely be a subjective impression gleaned from a single hearing, I cannot help wondering whether Boulez's recent works, laboring under the heavy burden of his past achievements, do not feed his ever-increasing energy into a creative mechanism of steadily waning powers. Do these works have some deep, secret weakness to conceal beneath the myriad of subtle details that adorn and, above all, *differentiate* them? This differentiation is so meticulous in fact that it is as though Boulez were actually afraid of one work's resembling another!

For, though nothing of the sort seemed to threaten the electrifying composer of the Second Piano Sonata, Boulez's present development leads one to fear he might turn into a pure stylist. The care he takes to mark each new work with its own particular stamp is also applied on a smaller scale to the individual pieces that compose each work. His respect for unity thus enters into conflict with a need for stylistic masks, with the result that these masks become all the more obvious. In *Le Marteau sans Maître* (as in *Le Visage Nuptial*), each of the

FIG. 17*

nine sections employs a different instrumental combination; only twice are the full resources of the orchestra brought into play. These resources are so limited however—flute, viola, xylorimba, vibraphone, guitar, and percussion—that the variety of instruments used in the different pieces does not make for any appreciable diversification of the work's sound-fabric, but

---

* Pierre Boulez, *Improvisation sur Mallarmé.* Copyright © 1958 by Universal Edition (London) Ltd. Reprinted by permission of the above and their agents: Universal Edition A. G., Vienna and Associated Music Publishers, Inc., New York.

merely produces a growing sense of poverty. In 1912, it was possible for Schönberg, who was still operating in a linear perspective, to consider differentiating the various sections of *Pierrot Lunaire* in this way, but one is very surprised to find that forty years later, and after having taken such an active part in the elimination of polyphonic linearity, Boulez should be capable of reviving such a discredited idea.

Le Marteau sans Maître contains other features that probably stem from stylistic intentions as well, but which are in contradiction with the principle of discontinuity and detract, in the end, from the work's overall stylistic unity. Many listeners have been disturbed by the close resemblance between the soprano-flute duo in Part Three (*L'Artisanat Furieux*) and a similar section in *Pierrot Lunaire*. I, however, feel that Boulez's flippancy in this section has more serious implications. The disjunct motion of the melodic line, for example, is not enough to offset the impression of continuity and permanence resulting from the use of tone-color; this error is not unlike that committed by his disciples who, out of fidelity to Webern, perhaps, write so many quartets and quintets. In the first instrumental "commentary" on *Bourreaux de Solitude* (Part Two of *Le Marteau sans Maître*), the polyphony is dominated by a rhythmic figure which, though constantly varied, is composed entirely of equal time-values; this constitutes a startling breach of the principle of irrational rhythm. Even more surprising, though, is the fact that this figure is further stressed by the use of a single, obsessing tone-color—that of a drum; this persistent repetition would seem to constitute a revival, in hardly more acceptable form, of Messiaen's *ostinato*. Moreover, Boulez's clearly deliberate decision to use only two or three instruments from a fairly rich percussion section in each part of the work— with the exception of the last—results in a monotonous sonority which cannot be justified by any concern for "economy of means." But the high point in this kind of stylization occurs in the last section of the work, which is another setting of the poem *Bel Edifice et Pressentiments*, already sung in its entirety in Part Five; in this "second version," the soprano's delivery is more rapid and involves *sprechgesang*. Now, this re-exposition of the text cannot be considered as an *ossia*, since it must obligatorily be performed,[13] and, in any case, Boulez was not primarily concerned with chance or open itineraries when he composed *Le Marteau sans Maître*. It is hard to believe that a redundancy of this sort, which the poem itself in no wise justifies, could possibly stem from inviolable structural imperatives.

Must we interpret this series of stylistic stunts as a wry protest on the part of a *compositeur maudit* who has finally conceded to the public a work it can appreciate but who, in so doing, wreaks his vengeance on both work and public? His wish to stop writing purely experimental music was one thing; his desire to impose his views on the concert-stage, and not just in specialized reviews, was quite another. *Le Marteau sans Maître* was the first work in which he displayed a realistic attitude towards performing difficulties, paying attention to such minute details as "the staggered arrangement of the bongos in front of the percussion player"; if this score (which an experienced conductor with excellent musicians at his disposal can prepare for performance in less than a dozen rehearsals[14] was primarily conceived to be performed and applauded, it has achieved its goal. Its undeniable attractiveness as sheer sound has helped to dispel the reputation for hermeticism which had grown up about the composer of *Structures*. The predominant use of percussion instruments—of both determinate and indeterminate pitch—the acid arabesques of plucked strings set against the fluidity of flute and voice and the medium-low tessitura of the rest of the orchestral apparatus all help to define

---

[13] This is true only insofar as the work is given in its entirety. For indeed, the composer allows excerpts from this score to be performed in public (cf. Vega Record, no. C30A66).

[14] Considering that we are dealing with a contemporary work lasting thirty-five minutes, this is a very modest figure.

an aural coloring which is not unlike that of Far Eastern music. One wonders whether this is purely coincidental, or whether one must once more criticize the stylist in Boulez (while paying tribute, in this case, to his sense of tact). Was he, like Stravinsky and Messiaen, merely trying to enlist the aid of non-European music? Boulez's keen interest in Asian musical traditions and his constant desire to hasten every form of convergency lead me to believe that he had more far-reaching intentions. To be the first to achieve that fusion of two traditions which certain excellent minds feel is the necessary end result of our culture—indeed, of all civilization—was a goal worthy of Boulez's ambitions. But if this was the case, one is forced to admit that *Le Marteau Sans Maître* falls far short of a goal which will, I feel, prove beyond the reach of twentieth-century artists in any case. Nevertheless, a failure of this sort would attest to the greatness of Boulez's work as a whole; for here the most immediately successful aspects are not necessarily the most important.

A Serial Poetics

At the time of Webern's death in 1945, Western music was at a standstill. The crisis of the musical language had reached fatal proportions. The disappearance of the powerful tonal syntax had encouraged a tendency to anarchy which Schönberg's arithmetic was too weak to combat with any real success. The more demanding composers found they could not accept any of these shams, and some preferred to retire into silence. Pierre Boulez's extraordinary precocity saved him from this paralysis. He may have been the first to realize that the twelve-tone row was both necessary and insufficient, that it did not constitute a definitive answer to modern formal problems, and that it provided only one co-ordinate of a more complex space which had still to be conquered. Restrictions sometimes prove, in the long run, to be creative; had Boulez lacked that "negating rigor" of his, he would not have been able to undertake, two years later, a systematic revision of the musical universe.

An authentic composer is a rare phenomenon in any case—none had appeared since Webern—but when that composer possessed the organizational gifts required by his historical moment, his appearance is especially significant. To my mind, Boulez's early works remain the most important part of his vast output; more vigorously, perhaps, than those of Webern—and certainly with greater finality—they implied a condemnation of every shade of neoclassicist: symphonists, folklore specialists, back-handed tonalists, and fabricators of still-born modes. Displaying, in the forties, an uncommon degree of optimism, Boulez sought and found, in the very failures of his elders, a justification for his belief that a reconstruction of musical language was imminent. In 1952, taking stock of his experience, he was able, not without a certain amount of pride, to endorse that condemnation—(*"Any composer who has not felt—I do not say understood, but felt—the necessity of the twelve-tone language is SUPERFLUOUS. For everything he writes will fall short of the necessities of his time"*)—and to confirm that optimism (*"henceforth, then, what is left for us but to attempt to gather up the fascicle of available possibilities elaborated by our predecessors, demanding of ourselves a minimum of constructive logic?"*) in terms of the results achieved in the interval (*"as opposed to convergent or divergent tone-rows, I have established the network of possibilities which was my goal. There now exists a conception of composition which need no longer refer back to the classical structures, not even to destroy them. I feel that it is now possible to move unimpeded toward a highly authentic form of being which, in its autonomy, will no longer need to repudiate anything whatsoever."*).[15]

In this last paragraph, Boulez was referring to his most deci-

---

[15] Pierre Boulez: "Eventuellement."

sive achievement, the elevation of the role of rhythm through the discovery of a process of rhythmic variation that acts as a catalyst on ever-shifting row-structures. This was the turning-point; this was where the world of "athematic" and discontinuous music really began. Five years later, the composer turned his attention to completely different problems and observed that present-day music "makes increasing use of notions that are variable in their very formulation and that are functions of ever-evolving hierarchies. This is why," he added, "we have seen the row of twelve equal tones replaced by rows of block-sonorities, the densities of which are never the same, why we have seen metrics replaced by the row of durations and block-rhythms (either rhythmic cells or several superposed time-values) and why we have seen the parameters of intensity and tone-color outgrow their decorative and emotional virtues and, without losing these privileged attributes, go on to acquire a functional significance that has increased both their powers and dimensions."[16] The reign of ambiguity had begun, giving the lie to those for whom "the repetition of an *audible* structure," as Michel Fano has put it, determines "whether or not a work is constructed." The rule set forth by Ruskin—"one thing must overshadow all the rest, by its size, by its function or by its interest"—has simply vanished, together with all the rules that were supposed to govern our sense of form until the end of time. The great classical works were the fruit of an architectural approach to music, and as such they made no secret of their structural patterns; the modern work conceals its structures in a network of countless subterranean channels.

"Gather up the fascicle. . .": with this phrase, which has such a curiously modest ring coming from him, Boulez summed up the historical situation that he has helped to unravel. There were useful elements scattered throughout the works of the masters; someone had to realize that these elements converged,

---

[16] Pierre Boulez, "Aléa," p. 853.

had to make their convergency a reality and re-interpret them collectively, even at the risk of destroying them, if their destruction would allow for a transcendency. On the whole, Boulez faced squarely up to these difficult problems. It was he who brought to light the post-Webernian notion which consists in doing away with thematic functions. He took the semantic role away from the theme, which had held it for so long, and gave it to ever-evolving rhythmic structures, dissociated at last from melody. He justified the Viennese composers' hyper-disjunct motion by incorporating it into a rhythmic and melodic concept, the basis of which is discontinuity. The absolute-counterpoint advocated by Schönberg was possible only through very great rhythmic freedom; the notion of irrational rhythm helped to dispel the harmonic implications normally found in all forms of polyphony. The face of music was being transformed along with its actual fabric. While a new, coherent technique was being elaborated, the outlines of something far more essential were also beginning to emerge, something which neither Schönberg nor even Webern were able to elaborate: *a serial poetics.*

"In order to create an effective sense of poetic delirium," proclaims Boulez, "we must consider delirium *per se* and, yes, organize it." Thus far, I feel, Boulez's actual works have not adequately fulfilled his splendidly over-ambitious intentions. In his experimental works, he gave free reign to his genius and, so long as the organization of a new language took precedence over every other goal, he was powerfully aided by his thirst for discovery. Over the years, however, this same thirst may well have become a hindrance that prevents his achieving his aesthetic aims. In contemporary music, each work is so utterly unique, in both form and intention, that it probably needs a very long "gestation period," a patient ripening, before its contours are set down on paper; if so, then one may wonder whether Boulez does not compose too much, whether he takes the necessary time he should to explore the farthest depths of those chasms the outlines of which his amazing musical intellect is often the first to glimpse. The reason behind Boulez's failure on the level of musical poetics—a failure which should normally have been spared him by virtue of his total success on the technical level—may lie in his excessive haste to compose.

It would be absurd to speculate on the future of an artist like Pierre Boulez, especially as he is just over thirty-five. Let me simply say that the scope of his accomplishments to date, though it may not afford a justification for the works themselves—nothing can help a work of art—nevertheless suffices to rank this French composer as one of the greatest precursory figures in Western art and thought, one of those men without whom things would not be what they are.

". . . The mere existence of the Brentano cycle had made some impression, and Adrian's name had begun in the inner circles of the art to have a certain esoteric and tentative fame. . . ."

These are the words in which Thomas Mann describes the birth of that mysterious thing called celebrity. He is referring to the composer-hero of his *Doctor Faustus* who, in his late twenties, began to find that a few people were already fascinated by his work, even though he, personally, had done nothing to attract public attention.

Mann, of course, is at liberty to speak of such an early stage in an artist's career; here it is he who is the actual artist, he who shapes the character's fate, or at any rate, knows what is in store for him, for his hero is already dead when the novel begins and the narration of his life entrusted to a third person.

I am not sure whether I have the same right to anticipate the prospects of a young composer and his music. A premature judgment is always a gamble, but in this case I am prepared to gamble. Ever since the first performance of *Séquence*, given at a Domaine Musical concert on March 10, 1956, the name of the French composer Jean Barraqué has acquired, in the "inner circles of the art" that "tentative fame" referred to by Mann (though Barraqué's fame will have to grow a good deal before it reaches the attention of a larger public). Despite the fact that so far his complete works consist of but a few hundred pages of manuscript, a number of musicians already consider Barraqué's music the most important contribution to their art since Debussy. I, for one, am tempted to rank it even higher. No one should be surprised, therefore, at my devoting an entire chapter of this book to a "reconnaissance" of Barraqué's universe, especially as there exist recordings of the young master's first three works to which the reader may refer, and though not, of course, definitive, they do nevertheless constitute courageous and praiseworthy ventures.

CHAPTER EIGHT

Jean Barraqué

Biographical Notes

At the present time it would be quite senseless to draw up a detailed biography of Jean Barraqué. Future critics will probably be more interested in the day-to-day manifestations of his extraordinary personality than in the few salient events that have marked the first thirty years of his solitary existence, devoted solely to music. Barraqué was born in Paris on January 17, 1928; he turned to music at the age of fifteen, while finishing his studies at the Lycée Condorcet. He studied harmony and counterpoint with Jean Langlais and from 1948 until 1951 regularly attended Olivier Messiaen's class in musical analysis at the Conservatory. He did not, however, enroll in any of the composition classes taught there by other professors. During this period he wrote not only his first twelve-tone compositions —which he does not wish to make public—but also the first version of *Séquence* (1950) and preliminary sketches for the Piano Sonata (1950–1952).

In October, 1951, Barraqué decided to acquaint himself with the new techniques of "music for tape" and, together with Pierre Boulez, Michel Philippot, Yvette Grimaud, and myself, attended a laboratory course offered by the Research Group for *Musique Concrète* of the Radiodiffusion-Télévision Française in their headquarters on the Rue de l'Université. Before definitively breaking with the Group—in July of 1954—he devised a short *Étude,* which constituted his only creative effort between 1952 and 1955. After this period of silence, he returned to composition in the summer of 1955, bringing *Séquence* to completion.[1] The following year he decided to undertake what is intended to be his life's work, *La Mort de Virgile,* based on *The Death of Virgil,* by the Austrian novelist Hermann Broch.

Though little inclined to express himself other than through music, Barraqué has published a number of discerning critical articles and essays on aesthetics in various reviews. He is now preparing an essay on Debussy which, like everything he writes, will reveal indirectly perhaps as much about himself and his work as about his subject. He has also given classes in musical analysis, and though unfortunately far too private, these have enabled a privileged few to become acquainted with his highly provocative exegeses on the works of Mozart, Debussy, Webern, and the composer whom he most reveres, Beethoven. Let us hope the day will come when one of these disciples will publish, in more accessible form, Barraqué's analysis of Beethoven's Fifth Symphony, Webern's Piano Variations, or his especially remarkable analysis of *La Mer.*

---

[1] In addition to these three recorded scores, Barraqué has written *Le Temps Restitué* (1956–1957) for voices and orchestra, never as yet performed, and ...*Au-dela du Hasard* (1959), for four groups of instruments and one of singers; this work was first performed in the Domaine Musical Series in Paris, on January 26th, 1960, with Pierre Boulez conducting.

Séquence *and the Great Lyrical Tradition in Singing*

Scored for soprano, piano, harp, violin, 'cello, celesta, glock-enspiel, vibraphone, xylophone and percussion,[2] *Séquence* was the first work which Barraqué consented to have performed in public. Most of it was composed in 1950, but it was re-worked and orchestrated in 1955 (the instrumental interludes, in particular, were added during this second stage of composition). Originally, the vocal part consisted of texts by Rimbaud and Paul Eluard, but in 1955 Barraqué replaced these with four poems by Nietzsche, of which the French titles are *Trois Fragments, Musique du Midi, De la Pitié,* and *Plainte d'Ariane.*[3]

The following simplified table shows the plan of *Séquence* and gives the French text of Nietzsche's poems:

I

Instrumental Introduction

First Canto

a) *Trois Fragments*

Bonheur! le plus beau des butins!
Toujours près, jamais assez,
Toujours demain, jamais aujourd'hui—
Ton chasseur te paraît-il trop jeune?
Es-tu vraiment le chemin du péché?
  De tous les péchés
Le plus agréable débordement?

---

[2] The celesta and glockenspiel are played by a single musician, as are the vibraphone and xylophone. The many percussion instruments employed require three more players, so that all told the conductor has ten performers under his direction.

[3] The original titles of these poems are: *Drei Bruchstücke, Musik des Südens, Vereinsamt* (a portion of *Mitleid hin und her*), and *Klage der Ariadne* (from *Also Sprach Zarathustra*).

Le tonnerre gronde sur la région,
La pluie tombe goutte à goutte:
Au pédant loquace dès le matin
Rien ne ferme la bouche.
A peine le jour se glisse-t-il par la fenêtre,
J'entends déjà la litanie!
L'averse tombe: prêcheuse, elle enseigne
Que tout — est vain.

Le jour décline, le bonheur et la lumière se dorent,
Midi est déjà loin.
Combien de temps encore? Alors la lune et les étoiles
Se lèveront avec le vent et le givre.
Je ne veux plus tarder.

b) Instrumental Parenthesis

c) *Musique du Midi*

Maintenant tout m'est échu en partage
Ce que jamais mon aigle a entrevu—:
Si bien des espoirs se sont évanouis,
—Ton harmonie me touche telle une fléche,
Baume de l'oreille et des sens,
Pour moi descendu du ciel.

Si tu peux diriger le désir de tes vaisseaux
Vers les côtes méridionales, les îles bienheureuses,
Le jeu des nymphes grecques, ah! n'hésite pas!—
Jamais aucun vaisseau ne trouva but plus beau!

II

First Instrumental Interlude

Second Canto

De la Pitié

D'un vol bruissant, ils s'en vont vers la ville,
Les corbeaux croassants;
Bientôt il va neiger—
Heureux celui à qui reste . . . une patrie!
Tu t'arrêtes figé,
Tu regardes en arrière, depuis combien de temps!
Es-tu donc fou
De fuire dans le monde . . . avant l'hiver?
Le monde . . . une porte ouverte
Sur mille déserts muets et froids!
Celui qui a perdu
Ce que je perdis ne s'arrête nulle part.
Tu t'arrêtes tout pâle,
Condamné à errer en plein hiver,
Pareil à la fumée
Qui cherche sans cesse des cieux plus froids.
Fuis, oiseau; râle
Ton chant sur le mode du désert!—

III

Second Instrumental Interlude

Third Canto

Plainte d'Ariane

Qui me réchauffe, qui m'aime encore?
Donnez des mains chaudes!
Donnez des coeurs réchauds!
Etendue, frissonante,
pareille au moribond à qui l'on chauffe les pieds—
secouée, hélas! de fièvres inconnues.
Tremblante devant les glaçons aigus des frimas,
    chassée par toi, pensée!

Innomable! Voilée! Effrayante!
   derrière les nuages!
foudroyée par toi,
oeil moqueur qui me regarde dans l'obscurité
   ainsi je suis couchée,
je me courbe et je me tords, tourmentée
par tous les martyrs éternels,
   frappée
par toi, chasseur le plus cruel,
toi le dieu—inconnu. . . .

Ah! Ah! tu t'approches
en rampant au milieu de cette nuit
que veux-tu, parles
Tu me pousses et me presses
Ah! tu es déjà trop près!
tu m'entends respirer, tu épies mon coeur
Jaloux que tu es
de quoi donc es-tu jaloux

Ote-toi

Pourquoi cette échelle
Veux-tu entrer
t'introduire dans mes pensées les plus secrètes

Impudent! Inconnu, Voleur!
Que veux-tu voler?
Que veux-tu écouter?
Que veux-tu extorquer,
toi qui tortures!
toi—le dieu-bourreau! . . . .

En vain!
Frappe encore! . . .
Toi le plus cruel des chasseurs!
ton prisonnier le plus fier,

brigand derrière les nuages . . .
parle enfin,
toi qui te caches derrière les éclairs! Inconnu! Parle!
Que veux-tu, toi qui guettes sur les chemins . . .
Comment?
Une rançon?
Que veux-tu comme rançon?
Demande beaucoup—ma fierté te le conseille!
et parle brièvement—c'est le conseil de mon autre
    fierté! . . .

. . . .

Parti! Il a fui lui-même, . . .
mon grand ennemi, . . .

Non! Reviens! O Reviens! . . .
mon dernier bonheur!

—Sois prudente, Ariane! . . .
Je suis ton labyrinthe . . .

           (*French translation by Henri Albert*)

The work is to be played without pauses.

Séquence is not a cantata; nor is it a chamber work, in the strict sense of the term. Neither is it, like *Pierrot Lunaire* or *Le Marteau sans Maître,* an instrumental suite built around a sung or spoken text. This unique score can best be likened to a concerto for a group of soloists, since even the soprano part receives an almost instrumental treatment and is hardly more important than the piano or violin parts which gravitate about it. In choosing poems by Nietzsche, Barraqué merely wished to pay tribute to patterns of thought and sensibility which he feels are very close to his own. It is interesting to note that he did his own rather free adaptation of a French translation. Many listeners are disconcerted by Barraqué's prosody, for it is not enough to say that he breaks up his phrases; he tears them word from word, quite literally atomizes them. He has no qualms about treating the French syllable as purely phonetic raw material, bringing out the "percussive properties" of certain consonants. This technique accentuates the impression of musical delirium which stems, on another level, from the constant changes of register and contrasts of intensity.

Still, there is nothing systematic in his approach; he often resorts to a prosody close to that of Debussy. In practice, however, the vocal line moves with such utter freedom that it constantly challenges any restrictive definition. For example, the syllabic structure of the first part of the phrase on which the soprano makes her entrance after the second instrumental interlude is quite classical, almost conventional (Fig. 18): but a change of tempo, sharp accents, and a rise in both tessitura and intensity transform the second part of the phrase into an impassioned cry which provides a strong contrast with the plaintive character of what comes before. This passage seems to capture the essence of the rapid, almost simultaneous fluctuations of the human soul; it is this impression that justifies—and, most likely, explains—the sudden change in the prosodic style, which becomes jerky, feverish, and seemingly erratic. As we shall see, Barraqué's entire poetic vision is based upon these sudden breaks in the equilibrium.

FIG. 18

This kind of correlation between the prosody and the secret, inner currents of both words and music is a constant factor in Barraqué's vocal writing. One of the work's loveliest passages occurs at the end of *Musique du Midi;* the last lines of the poem are cut up into short, choppy fragments and are murmured by the soprano in such disconnected fashion that she seems choked with emotion, barely able to articulate the words, which rise to her lips as though wrenched from the depths of silence: *"ja . . . mais . . . aucun . . . vaisseau . . . netrou . . . va . . . but-plusbeau . . ."* (see Fig. 23).

The opening lines of the following canto lie at the opposite end of the poetic scale; here the sporadic, hasty delivery takes on an entirely different meaning (Fig. 19). The passage begins

FIG. 19

in a "very declamatory" style, then sinks, during the third and fourth measures, to a "whisper" (these are the indications on the score); abruptly there follows a kind of "outcry," then a spoken passage to be delivered in a "dry, rather shrill" tone, and the style finally becomes declamatory again on the words *"Tu t'arrêtes figé."* Barraqué is a composer of such noble breed that he cannot be suspected of any descriptive intentions here, and listeners who might be tempted to interpret the vocal arabesque at the beginning of this period as the sign of a "dramatic" sensibility, or to dwell upon the "anecdotal" side of a phrase in which the idea of flying crows (*"d'un vol bruissant ils s'en vont vers la ville"*) is associated with a three-fold image of falling curves—melodic (from the highest to the lowest register), rhythmic (from sixteenth-note triplets to eighth-notes), and dynamic (from full-throated singing to a whisper)—would probably be reading more into the score than the composer had intended.

I would rather not attempt to give Barraqué's vocal style a "close reading"; I would prefer merely to call attention to its very wide expressive range. There is, however, nothing to prevent my trying to ascertain the aesthetic motivations behind that style. For example, the soprano is told to *speak* the words *"celui à qui reste . . . une patrie,"* thus conferring upon this disclosure a parenthetical quality which is perfectly justified—both by the need for a rapid, indeed frantic, delivery, and by the unique pairing of the word *"Heureux"* with the apostrophe *"Tu t'arrêtes figé"* rather than by its actual meaning. But the climax of this phrase undoubtedly occurs during the outcry

FIG. 20

"Bientôt il va neiger—Heureux . . ." which rings out like a shriek of despair: tidings of evil that disrupt the atmosphere of bliss which has suffused the orchestra since the end of Section One. This same outcry turns up again near the end in a strangely identical form (this, I believe, is the one obvious repetition in the work) on the words *"Que veux-tu extorquer, toi qui . . .";* in this case it is preceded by a long silence tinged with dread and immediately followed by the key-word of the fourth poem, *"tortures";* in both cases the figure is undoubtedly meant to suggest the same feeling of extreme anguish and defiance. This helps to clarify, in the first example, the unique position of the word *"Heureux,"* which is handled in a kind of musical antiphrasis (Fig. 20).

The first note sung by the soprano in the Second Canto—a fortissimo G-sharp (cf. Fig. 19)—is the first of a series of forceful attacks employing the uppermost vocal register which are scattered throughout this section. Barraqué favors this note to the extent of invariably[4] allotting it the same function each time it appears: in the line mentioned above—*"TU t'arrêtes figé"*—a bit later as the first note of a descending *vocalise—"LE monde . . ."*—still later on *"TU t'arrête"* (this verse being delivered in a declamatory tone), and once again on the first shouted syllables of the line *"PAREIL À LA FUMÉE QUI CHERche sans cesse des cieux plus froids."* After that, this favored G-sharp appears only once more, on the word *"FRAPpée,"* in the Third Canto; the two remaining fortissimo attacks in this high register are both on G naturals. This frequent repetition of a single effect in such a short space of time raises the expressive intensity of this passage to a maximum, creating an almost unbearable tension. On the other hand, whenever the score indicates that a word is to be shouted, this effect is invariably set in a context designed to emphasize its "surprise" value. An example of this kind is found at the beginning of the Third Canto; the last syllable of the phrase *"Étendue, frissoNANTE,"* which comes at the end of a very subdued passage, is meant to be "shouted." A bit further on, the same is true of the interjection *"Ah! Ah!,"* which immediately precedes the words *"tu t'approches"*; the composer indicates that it should be "shouted without vibrato," even though it is pitched in a medium-low register, sliding from low B to middle C. A similar demand is made on the soprano in the First Canto: she is told to deliver the line *"les îles bienheureuses"* in a "fortissimo whisper." One of the work's most lyrical episodes—from *"Maintenant tout m'est échu en partage"* to *"Pour moi descendu du ciel"*—is alternately composed of carefully articulated instrumental passages, devoid of any vibrato, and snatches of full-throated singing which give free reign to the splendor of the human voice. All these notations, to-

---

[4] With one exception, however, four measures before the beginning of the second interlude.

gether with the other shades of expression customarily used in modern *Sprechgesang* technique—"parlando," "flautando," "comme parlé," "entre parlé et chuchoté," etc.—attest to Barraqué's constant need for expressive intensity and his passionate concern for poetic tension. These traits were already implicit in his choice of a text, and when they go hand in hand with such a keen ear for dramatic effect they are, I believe, the signs of a great lyric temperament.

If we go on to examine Barraqué's sumptuous vocal writing from the standpoint of melody, we discover further proof of this lyrical temperament. The flamboyant style of certain episodes in the *Ring, Erwartung* and, above all, in *Don Giovanni*, episodes which derive their magical effect from the fascinating power of large intervals, reaches its apotheosis in the disjunct vocal style of *Séquence*.[5] I doubt whether it is possible to handle the human voice with greater freedom; delicate vocal chords run a certain risk in taking on *Séquence* and well-known soloists have refused to sing the score once they have taken stock of the difficulties involved. Daring as it is, however, Barraqué's style always stops short of the unreasonable, for it is thoroughly *vocal;* he never asks the impossible, since he has a marvelous feeling for the human voice and an intuitive grasp of its possibilities. Unlike Webern in his Songs with Guitar and Clarinet, op. 18, everything that Barraqué demands of the voice falls within that great tradition of vocal lyricism which he has revived in a modern context, without once over-stepping its natural bounds.

The lines *"chassée par toi, pensée! Innomable! Voilée! Effrayante! derrière les nuages,"* provide the basis for one of those

---

[5] Though these references are no doubt historically justified, they nevertheless remain, in some ways, foreign to Barraqué's universe. Personally, the composer of ... *Au-delà du Hasard* is inclined to refer to the lyricism of Beethoven, and especially to the disjunct vocal writing of the *Missa Solemnis* (to name the work which he says most deeply influenced him).

purely vocal melodic curves (Fig. 21) which, though they do not allow the voice a real burst of lyricism, and may therefore seem rather colorless, nevertheless contain exceptional lyric potentialities. (In point of fact, the lyrical outburst is held back for some time to come, despite the ever-increasing violence of the orchestral pressure, and is finally released only a few measures before the end of the work.) The center of gravity of this phrase never strays far from the medium register, except for one skip into the bass on the word "*innomable*"; nevertheless, on either side of this central word the melodic line is highly dis-

FIG. 21

jointed, especially during the first half of the phrase when the intervals grow gradually larger (they tend to grow smaller toward the end). The beauty of the phrase lies, I feel, precisely in the fact that, despite its angularity, it never loses that sustained electrical charge which, we sense, must eventually touch off the delirious fireworks of ecstasy. Thus the composer has contrived to set up aesthetically necessary zones of tension, characterized by their static, and in a sense, negative quality, in anticipation of dimly perceptible things to come.

Finally the phrase falls away in a swift *decrescendo* (on "*les nuages*") combined with an upward melodic curve. This kind of ending is typical of Barraqué's vocal style, and there are frequent examples of it in *Séquence*. I have reason to feel that this "rising fall" is not simply a mannerism, but a deeply personal trait; it may even be one of those idiosyncracies which are unconsciously and lovingly cultivated by certain great composers and contain a small parcel of their poetic substance. For this reason, they are more than mere mechanical clichés; they fulfill the nobler function of a signature. It would seem that the tone-row upon which *Séquence* is based was conceived deliberately to allow for the melodic line to be left hanging in this way; these

FIG. 22a

"rising falls" take the form of ascending major sevenths or major ninths, culminate, not on unvoiced syllables but on prosodic accents, and are followed by pauses that are generally rather long. The work contains a good many examples of this type of writing, some in a tender mood (Fig. 22a), some more violent (Fig. 22b).

FIG. 22b

It is only superficially paradoxical to ascribe a large part of the unity of *Séquence*'s vocal style to those very elements of discontinuity on which it feeds. For indeed, the leaps in his disjunct style, the gaps in his breathless prosody, and the complex network of apparently conflicting attacks and dynamics are the woof on which Barraqué weaves the warp of a vocal discourse which becomes increasingly coherent with repeated hearings.

Séquence: *The "Orchestra-As-Instrument"*

The style of vocal lyricism which I have briefly attempted to describe may, for some time, continue to be considered the outstanding feature of *Séquence*. My own feeling, however, is that as time goes by, it is the orchestral writing, the relationships between voice and instruments and, above all, the work's overall structure which will excite even greater wonder and admiration.

Barraqué's conception of instrumentation deserves a closer examination which, unfortunately, is beyond the scope of this essay. He has broken with Webern's asceticism which, though necessary at one period in musical history, would have placed drastic limits on the universe of serial music had it been carried any farther. Barraqué wishes to enlarge that universe as much as possible, just as he is working to increase the expressive range of the human voice. His efforts have already resulted in one important contribution: the instrumental ensemble is no longer handled as a chamber group; it assumes an ambivalent role, acting alternately as an "orchestra-as-instrument" and as a group of individual soloists.

First let us consider the "orchestra-as-instrument": *Séquence* provides the first example in Western music of a *functional* orchestra, that is one in which each tone-color is stripped of its individuality and exists only *as a function* of its relationship to the other tone-colors used in the same structure; this relationship can be of a simultaneous nature, *but it can also be sequential*. The orchestra thereby becomes a huge, single instrument, endowed with such varied possibilities of sound-production that when these are exploited to the utmost they create the impression of a perpetual bursting apart within the framework of

an absolute unity. Thus, in the first interlude, after a piano episode written in an angular, profusely accented style reminiscent
of the Piano Sonata, the tension which, until this point, has not
been exteriorized, bursts forth in a brief percussion solo, then
sinks below the surface again while the orchestra begins de-
veloping a commentary of great complexity. Here we have a
kind of musical osmosis: the tone-color of each instrument is
diffused in every direction, setting up an incessant flow of mutual exchanges. The resultant counterpoint is composed of several undefined parts in which all the elements cross and mingle,
intertwine and then disentangle themselves again, in such a way
that the ear is never quick enough to grasp the nature of the relationships governing this polyphony. An instrumental ensemble transformed into a polymorphous instrument contains
within itself the very principle of its discontinuity.

But the orchestra in *Séquence* is also a *group of individual
soloists*. The apparent supremacy of the vocal line is often challenged by instrumental passage-work in cadenza-like style;
solos of this kind are continually breaking away from the "orchestra-as-instrument," only to be re-absorbed by it almost immediately. They are like splendid geysers gushing forth now
and again, whenever the underlying tension becomes too great.
There are violin cadenzas which seem to be drawn from some
never-to-be-written concerto—never to be written because the
very principle of the orchestra-as-instrument precludes the
concerto form; piano cadenzas introducing dialogues with the
vocal part, or else unleashing, in a few aggregations of notes,
the pent-up fury accumulated in the course of an interlude:
over-flowing passion is the key to the entire work.

In these cadenzas, as in many other passages of *Séquence*,
Barraqué's instrumental writing is almost dangerously daring. It
has been claimed that certain passages in the violin and 'cello
parts, passages which contain harmonics, are practically impossible to play. In order to give this opinion fair appraisal, we
must bear in mind that most instrumentalists, even the best of

them, tend to be naturally lazy: Beethoven often came up against this sort of cautious conservativism. Nevertheless, some of the criticisms leveled against the instrumental writing in *Séquence* may be perfectly justified. In that case, we must hope that the composer will consent to revise a few details of his brilliant and resourceful instrumentation which, though it boldly takes virtuosity for granted, does so at considerable risk. (Barraqué has, in fact, already altered certain figures for the harp, and contemplated doing away with a few percussion instruments.)

The same kind of virtuosity also turns up in the percussion parts. The three percussion players have eighteen different types of instrument to divide up amongst them: timpani, snaredrum, tenor drum, tom-tom, bass-drum, tambourine, ordinary cymbals, high-hat cymbals, Chinese crash cymbal, gong, claves, castanets, wood-block, temple blocks, maracas, triangle, cenceros, and whip. Or rather, they have to *take turns* playing these instruments, for here the percussion parts are by no means fixed, as they are in Messiaen's scores which assign an instrument—or group of instruments—to each musician for a given period of time. Based as they are on a wide diversity of tone-color, the percussion parts in *Séquence* require the players to change instruments continually, and this gives rise to rather ticklish problems of distribution. However, this shifting about is *not* gratuitous; it is the result of a conscious effort to achieve a series of ever-changing accoustical effects. It is the very essence of the orchestral conception under discussion.

Nonetheless, Barraqué, unlike Edgar Varèse, does not give the percussion instruments a preponderant aesthetic role. In Barraqué's work the percussion generally remain in the background, effectively contributing to enrich the texture of the musical discourse. At several points in the score, however, they do leap to the fore, either to take their turn as chief element of the accompaniment (as at the end of the Second Canto: "*Fuis, oiseau . . .*") or to burst out, like their fellow instruments, in luxuriant cadenzas (as after the piano solo in the first interlude or at the end of the tensest episode in the Third Canto: *"Reviens mon dernier bonheur"*); they may also perform short solos (the most noteworthy percussion solo comes in near the very beginning of the work and employs three temple blocks, the maracas and claves, with a sustained tremolo on the celesta in the background). Barraqué's genius for handling tone-color is most brilliantly evident in the way he combines the percussion with the so-called "melodic" instruments. He has devised associations and contrasts of an unprecedented subtlety. One splendid example of this occurs in the brief orchestral passage which links *Trois Fragments* with *Musique du Midi*. The economy of means in the scoring of this passage is exemplary: a trio composed of the tom-tom, cenceros, and claves is accompanied by very simple figures played alternately on the harp and piano. From time to time these two groups are highlighted by single fleeting notes from the glockenspiel or the vibraphone, or by pizzicati in the 'cello.

The overall "morphology" of the work is determined by a dialectical play between the solo cadenza style on the one hand, and the discontinuous style of what we have dubbed the "orchestra-as-instrument," on the other. No other piece of music, I believe, has yet demonstrated better than *Séquence* the extraordinarily effective role which the tone-color phenomenon plays in authentic serial music; not only does it establish the work's definitive coloration, as in the classical conception, but it seems to reveal the work's every contour and even its most secret, inner flux. Strangest of all, however, is the fact that a single score, a single "pre-orchestral score for piano"[6] can contain the germ, not of several different orchestrations but, as Barraqué himself has stated, of several different *works*. Thus, once tone-color *per se* becomes as important a component of

---

[6] I am, of course, purposely simplifying problems of a highly complex nature.

music as the order of the notes and the ways in which they are superposed, it is then in a position to free itself from the other components and, through them, to become the material for another work, a "work of the second degree," as it were. This new work would be related to the original one, since the schema of notes and rhythms is still the same, but would also be sufficiently independent of the original so as not to be pre-conditioned by it. Ambiguity carried this far in the creative process would be clear proof that music is the most modern of the arts, and perhaps even—why not put it bluntly?—the only art that truly represents our time.

In order to appreciate music which is so organically associated with the tone-color phenomenon, we must leave traditional notions of orchestration and instrumentation behind us. The key to the "morphology" of *Séquence* lies, above all, in the relationship between the various instruments and the vocal part. This relationship is always contrapuntal; but while this counterpoint sometimes assumes a fairly accessible linear shape, its more subtle forms are involved with the concept of *Klangfarbenmelodie*, and are more difficult to grasp. When, in the First Canto, the singer attacks the line, "*Ton chasseur te paraît-il trop jeune*," the piano answers her in a very linear dialogue (though the play of attacks and intensities does give it a certain discontinuity). Almost immediately the celesta joins in, followed by the harp, and finally by the strings, which move in tighter and tighter patterns until they seem to disintegrate in the dust-shower of a *spicatto* on the words: "*goutte à goutte*." In the first few measures following the words "*Tu regardes en arrière*" in the Second Canto, a more disjointed, though equally linear counterpoint is woven by the five parts: piano, harp, violin, 'cello, and soprano. But it is in the Third Canto, starting with the words "*ainsi je suis couchée*," that this kind of writing becomes most complex; here all the instruments are involved in the counterpoint, creating an effect of increasing effervescence which culminates in the words *"toi le dieu—inconnu."* It is obviously impossible for the ear to follow any given instrumental part through polyphony as dense as this. The linear impression vanishes completely, leaving only a sparkling multitude, a circle rotating at such high speed as to create the illusion of fixity.

Thus, through completely different channels, the extremely linear character of this passage results in the same kind of immobility in which the work originates. Over and above the inextricable give and take of the counterpoints, we again encounter, in a more complex form, the spirit of the *Klangfarbenmelodie*, whose downfall had seemed to be the inevitable result of this new technique of instrumentation. Conversely, it is possible to find contrapuntal meaning in a passage whose scoring might seem to be no more than a purely poetic use of the *Klangfarbenmelodie*, a sort of iridescence surrounding the vocal line (Fig. 23): such are the paradoxes of contemporary musical language!

FIG. 23

Form and the Tone-Row in Séquence

In its twelve-tone conception, *Séquence* is typical of the period in which it was written, the early fifties. At that time young European composers were primarily concerned with casting off the formal strictures which Webern had, on the contrary, sought to consolidate in works like the Quartet, op. 28; but they also wished to find more satisfactory solutions than those which merely circumvented the problem. The melodic and harmonic texture of *Séquence* derives from two rows, the first of which (Fig. 24a) gives rise, through a rather complex system of analogies, to the second (Fig. 24b).

FIG. 24a

Disregarding the first three measures—these constitute a section apart in which several versions of both rows are used simultaneously—the first part of the work employs only the first row, the second part derives from the second row, while the third and last part makes alternate use of both. To each of these rows there corresponds a separate and distinct musical universe which is partly defined by it. The second interlude, however, does contain a "parenthetical" section which combines both rows in a highly original kind of interplay, creating a new form of musical filigree.

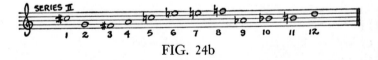

FIG. 24b

In choosing the intervals which determine the structure of a row, a composer commits himself irrevocably. It is absurd to claim that this choice is arbitrary and cannot affect the success or failure of the composition. On the contrary, it seems obvious to me that the textural richness—or penury—of any given passage in a score is determined by this choice. Hence, the true row composer should be capable of establishing a direct, anticipatory contact with the future development of his work from its very inception. In order that the unique raw material which he will have at his disposal be perfectly adapted to the needs of creative thinking, he must have a clear, aural impression of the work as a whole from the very outset. This will enable the parts to act upon the whole in a kind of backlash effect that calls to mind the fascinating perspectives revealed by modern biology.

It is impossible, of course, for the musical analyst to pass a value judgment on the choice of a row; this would be as sense-less as criticizing an athlete's physique. All I can do is to list the intervals that go to make up the row, expressing them in arithmetical terms.[7] The two rows employed in *Séquence* may be set forth in two groups of figures (Fig. 25).

	1	2	3	4	5	6	7	8	9	10	11	12
SERIES I	+11	+2	+7	+11	+2	+1	+6	+1	+9	+4	+9	
SERIES II	+6	+11	+3	+3	+3	+1	+1	+3	+2	+1	+3	

FIG. 25

The relationships between these two rows are of an inter-structural nature, and would require a fairly long analysis to define. I can, however, call attention to a few points of com-parison between them. The first row does not contain the inter-val +3 (ascending major third); but if we bear in mind that the interval +9 is its inversion (major sixth), and that the inversion of the interval +11 (major seventh) is +1 (minor second), the first four notes of the second row are seen to bear an obvious relationship to the seventh, eighth, ninth, and tenth notes of the first row. The chief difference between the two rows lies in the wider range of possibilities afforded by the first, for, taking into account all the possible inversions, it contains every interval of the chromatic scale, whereas the major third (+4),

---

[7] This system of row notation serves to identify each interval —always considered as ascending—by the number of half tones it contains.

the perfect fourth (+5), and their inversions (+8 and +7) are missing from the second.

The second row, because it begins with an augmented fourth (+6) and also because of the diminished seventh chord formed by the series of minor thirds (+3) from notes three to six, affords opportunities for consonant note-groups which the composer makes no effort to avoid. Similarly, he allows himself, toward the end of the work, to score one of the soprano's most moving cries—*"Que veux-tu comme rançon? Demande beaucoup"*—as a sort of E major-minor cadence (Fig. 26).

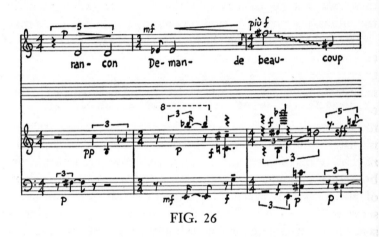

FIG. 26

Dogmatic disciples of Webern will undoubtedly disapprove of this "tonal throwback," but Barraqué, like every true serial composer, has nothing but contempt for an attitude which, though it was of some use at a time when the sense of tonality was still strong, was destined to be but a temporary and, in the end, uncreative taboo. Nor does Barraqué go along with the disciples of Schönberg in their fondness for dissonance at any price, and the choice of the intervals in the genetic rows of *Séquence* probably reflects his concern for sheer beauty in sound more than anything else. Philosophically, this may be a reactionary concept, but Barraqué has made it a basic consideration in all his music, bringing it up to date again with all the authority great works can wield.

For the critic, one of the most interesting aspects of *Séquence* is the absolute cohesion between the work's poetic essence and its use of the tone-row technique. I have already referred twice to the extraordinary beauty of the last measures in the First Canto. It is not uninteresting to note that this musical "fade-out" is obtained by a strict retrogradation of the rows found in the first measures. Here again, Barraqué seems to have discovered the unique poetic truth of a technique which has become extremely common ever since Schönberg first used it in the eighteenth piece of *Pierrot Lunaire*.

The second interlude, too, culminates in a passage whose exceptional poetic qualities demanded an exceptional use of the twelve-tone technique. This interlude may be regarded as the most significant—and probably the loveliest—passage in the entire work; here the musical discourse seems to move on a metaphysical level. The second interlude begins almost immediately after the last line of the Second Canto—*"Fuis, oiseau; râle ton chant sur le mode du désert"*—which is sung in a tone bordering on despair. In the space of only a few pages, a sense of temporal suspension gradually evolves which ultimately seems to abolish the time dimension altogether; it is as though some living organism had made the perilous effort of communicating its most secret spark of life, and then died.

The interlude begins with a brief duet between the celesta and 'cello. Other instruments creep into the polyphony and among them the piano, which soon soars up in a solo of paroxysmic trills. It is accompanied for a few measures by percussion instruments; then, at the moment of a cymbal crash, makes way for a brief violin cadenza, before returning to challenge, as it were, its stringed rival, finally drowning it out completely. But suddenly the proud, sumptuous lyricism of this passage is unseated, so to speak, by the poetic, "nocturnal" passage that follows (Barraqué's work abounds in reversals of this sort).

This passage consists of a rather long, extremely dense *tutti*, pierced by an occasional streak of light, and which produces that effect of sparkling fixity to which I have already referred in connection with a passage in the Third Canto.

This first part of the interlude paves the way for more exceptional moments to come. It is followed directly by a quartet episode—for xylophone, vibraphone, harp, and celesta—that displays an extraordinary economy of means. The tissue of sound becomes light and transparent; nothing remains but the tenuous, shimmering murmur of a scarcely audible conversation. We seem to be hovering above some unidentified territory.

Then an intruder bursts upon the scene. Like a foreign body hurtling down from another world, a single, violent piano chord, terrifying in its solitude, cuts brutally in on the ecstatic atmosphere which had gradually dissolved our sense of time. The passage inaugurated by this chord is set, we might say, "in different type"; now the feeling that we are out of time is at its height. While this resplendent six-note chord goes on endlessly vibrating with hypnotic fixity, the other six notes appear one by one at its side like so many points of light. Next, this miniature firmament seems to shift about, assuming a new shape which is structurally analogous to the first: a six-note chord surrounded by a constellation of the other six notes. Altogether, the two groups of six notes—the one vertical, the other horizontal—go through six different permutations of this kind. The chord takes on six separate and distinct forms, expressed in six different combinations of tone-color, each of which modifies, not only the coloring of the chord itself, but that of the melodic notes, as well. The chord is provided with another set of satellites, contributed by the percussion section, but even this is not enough to bridge the hermetic frontiers of this world within a world, linked to the rest of the work only through subtle, strictly serial analogies. For the parenthetical quality of this passage is due to a break in the dodecaphonic unity of the work. Neither of its genetic rows is used here in its entirety;

FIG. 27

instead, the composer alternately borrows elements from both rows, merging them in antagonistic symbiosis. None of the six chords properly belongs to either of the original rows; each constitutes an inversion of any of the other five, and the total effect of these inversions on the twelve-tone fabric is so powerful as to challenge the work's entire "morphological" conception, both past and future. This unique, splendidly strange middle-section, which is saved from absolute incongruity by the existence of a few, tenuous threads, towers out of the midst of a lyrical universe to which it seems absolutely foreign (Fig. 27).

This passage is followed abruptly by a very brief, fiery passage that resounds like a *tutti* for full orchestra;[8] though it seems to bring the passage to a crumbling end, it is actually the beginning of the introduction to the Third Canto (and, at the same time, the last phase of the interlude). Immediately the music breaks out of its state of suspended animation and the notion of time returns. All the forces which seemed to have died now struggle back to life.

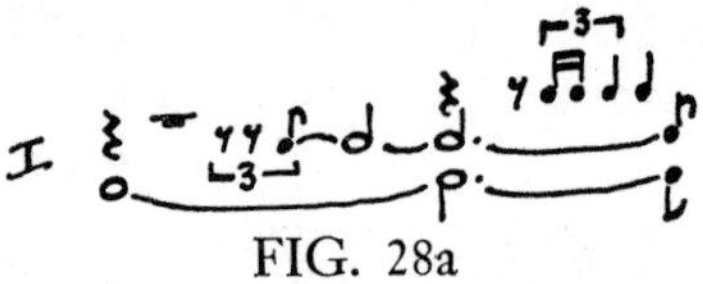

FIG. 28a

During this last part of the work the music will be constantly torn by a difficult choice between the restrained lyricism of Part One and the tumultuous excitement of Part Two. Each of these parts grew out of a rhythmic structure all its own, coupled in Part One with a slow tempo (Fig. 28a), and in Part Two with a faster one (Fig. 28b). A great many subtle variants of both these structures have recurred continually in the

---

[8] This is the only mass effect—achieved, incidentally, with only six instruments!—that I have been able to find in a work composed essentially of solos.

most unexpected shapes. Added to this has been the notion of *parenthesis*, which we encountered twice: first in the outcry "*Bientôt il va neiger—Heureux*," and again, much later on, in the second interlude. Here in the Third Canto, this notion of

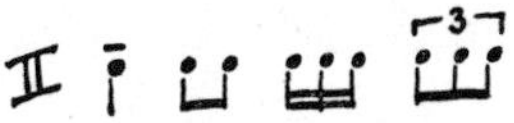

FIG. 28b

parenthesis acts as a catalyst in the interaction of two worlds, which are induced, by means of a truly splendid musical device, to exchange components, entering into a structural and poetic interplay. At the same time, sudden changes of tempo complete the disruption of the musical discourse by breaking it up into small fragments.

Séquence is one of those rare works in the history of music that quivers with an intense life of its own from start to finish. This quality is expressed in the form of unique "poetic moments," like those already described. The perpetual poetic diversity which the work derives from its formal richness should, I feel, be apparent even to listeners unfamiliar with contemporary musical idiom. In *Séquence*, there are very few obvious similarities between any two given moments. One such case has already been cited (the two "outcries" and their orchestral contexts); another, the only literal repetition in the entire work,[9] is the recurrence of the same melisma in two different cantos: on the soprano's entrance—"*Bonheur! le plus beau des butins*"—in the First, and on the words "*tortures! toi —le dieu-bourreau*" in the Third. Much more often, each moment is absolutely unique, related to the others only through the underlying unity of the work as a whole. Thus, the opening words of the Third Canto ("*Qui me réchauffe?*"), the first to

---

[9] It is also worth noting that the second appearances of these two fragments—the soprano's outcry and her first melisma—occur one right after the other, which, in itself, constitutes an exceptional situation.

be sung without orchestral accompaniment, constitute a unique moment in the work, a zone of expectancy which, poetically speaking, offers absolutely no point of comparison with the only other unaccompanied passage, *"oeil moqueur qui me regarde."* From a more general standpoint, however, static zones of this sort occur fairly frequently. They alternate, as we have already seen, with zones of expansion in a broad, asymmetrical pulsation which is a higher manifestation of the work's life-beat. In this respect, the very last measures of the work constitute a summit of musical expression; in the wake of that splendid cry *"Demande beaucoup,"* the orchestra musters all its strength to sustain the now gasping soprano and bear her upwards to her highest note; this she hits in the middle of the line *"O Reviens! MON dernier bonheur,"* only to be interrupted forthwith by a burst of percussion. This hiatus is followed by an even more extraordinary moment, for now the work has no alternative but to fade into silence in the space of only a few measures. The soprano, rejoining the instrumental pianissimo, sings the last, heart-rending lines: *"Sois prudente, Ariane! . . . Je suis ton labyrinthe."* This last syllable, incidentally, is accompanied by a brilliantly appropriate gong effect, nearly submerged by the reverberations of celesta, vibraphone, and crashing cymbal. Taken as a whole, this sequence of musical events constitutes an extraordinary farewell.

Thus ends this masterwork, probably the greatest piece of music written in Europe since Debussy's last period, and certainly the most rigorous, from an aesthetic standpoint. Yet so splendid a score as *Séquence*—which might also have taken its title from one of the Nietzsche poems used in it: *Musique du Midi*—is still practically unknown. As Proust once wrote: "It was Beethoven's quartets themselves that devoted half a century to forming, fashioning, and enlarging a public for Beethoven's quartets." It may take less time for *Séquence* to create its audience; despite its uncompromising purity, the work seems to have a certain direct appeal by virtue of its amazing beauty as sheer sound, a quality which was lacking in the Fifteenth Quartet.

The Piano Sonata

I have devoted so much space to a description of *Séquence* simply because it is by far Barraqué's most accessible work. But, though I, for one, feel that its role is closer to that of *The Afternoon of a Faun* than to that of *La Demoiselle Elue*, posterity may well regard it as an "early work." The same is not likely to be true of the Piano Sonata, begun only a few weeks after the completion of the first draft of *Séquence*. One is amazed to think that this towering score, which might easily be the musical testament of some venerable master, written at the end of a long career and at an age of solitary retirement and renunciation, should in fact be the work of a very young man. Certain works of Mozart and Schubert are astonishingly precocious; this one is terrifyingly so.

Like Beethoven's greatest sonatas, Barraqué's is conceived on a very large scale and lasts over half an hour. Its massiveness is that of a block of marble, and in some ways it has marble's glacial stillness, as well. It may be said to be divided into two parts, the first dominated by a rapid tempo and the second by a very slow one. But while the Sonata, like *Séquence*, is meant to be played without pauses, the demarcations are far less distinct here than in the earlier work. A comparison between these two works, which stem from a similar attitude toward composition, seems all the more relevant as they have certain elements—and particularly certain rhythmic elements—in common. (They may one day, in fact, share the same opus number in the catalogue of Barraqué's complete works.) The interrelationships between these two scores are, to my knowledge, without parallel in the history of music, but conversely no two works written by one and the same man have ever been so radically different. Superficially, one might say that their dissimilarity is one of rigor versus looseness. Yet though it is true that rigor is the keynote of the Sonata's style, certain sections of it—especially the very beginning—are handled in what is commonly known as a free style, while this same "free" style is occasionally abandoned in *Séquence*. The basic difference between the two scores is one of *mood*. *Séquence*, despite its "nocturnal" passages—perhaps the loveliest in the work—is life-giving, diurnal music. The Sonata, on the other hand, gradually descends into death; it is the Orphean work par excellence, inviting the listener on a journey to the Underworld from which there is no return.

For centuries the Western composer has delivered his message with the accents of faith. In a Bach chorale, which constitutes the highest expression of this attitude in art, the music *sings;* it is the music of confidence and love. Beethoven was the first to challenge his forefathers' serenity with such profoundly disturbing works as the Great Fugue. But Barraqué's Sonata actually succeeds in expressing disbelief; it is the first full-fledged expression in art of that grandiose sense of despair which has only been hinted at by literature. I wish to emphasize the Nietzschean aspects of this despair, preserved against any pernicious interpretation by its essential purity; a despair in which the Dionysian spirit reveals its most secret visage.

Here, for the first time in history, perhaps, Music comes face to face with her arch-enemy, Silence. In the early passages, Music's essentially dynamic character leaves no room for her enemy; but soon Silence begins to filter in. He first appears in insidious shapes, hollowing out tiny pockets in the mass of sound. Wherever a given structure lacks a note, who knows but what Silence has not spirited it away? But Music fights back: now she gathers herself in a solid mass, now she spreads herself out in registers and now, coiling up like a huge snake, she lies motionless for minutes on end, with only an occasional shiver to show that the work is still alive. Inexorably, however, Silence reappears in the shape of irrational pauses that grow steadily longer and more threatening in the course of an interminable development. If Music retaliates by donning the mask of her adversary and becoming Silence, then he in turn assumes the shape of Music. Caught up in a frenzy of expansion, the work breaks out of its fixity and hurries toward its close, in a series of "forgotten" developments and "implied" periods, monstrous musical ellipses, so to speak. Now Music musters all her strength once more to streak about in flights of unbearable lyricism; the notes bunch together and heave upward to form towering barriers, but these only succeed in deepening the furrows of silence at their feet. Then, for a moment, Music pauses to look back, in a fleeting effort to return to her origins; is there still time for a fresh start? But the adversary is close at hand. The finale attains a summit of agonizing grandeur; the relentless process is coming to an end now, and Music cracks under the inhuman strain, disintegrates and is sucked into the void. Whole slabs of sound crumble and vanish beneath the all-engulfing ocean of silence, until only the twelve notes of the row remain, and even these are plucked off, one by one.

Although this final passage of the Sonata attains the most ineffable beauty, it would be completely meaningless taken out of context. It recalls one of the greatest moments in Beethoven, a passage in the Eighth Quartet in which an equally simple structure—a major scale—was used to add an entirely new and precious dimension to the range of musical expression, a dimension which may well have been rapture itself.

For the moment this Sonata still defies any real analysis. It is unclassifiable, incomparable and, to some degree, still incommunicable music. We may rest assured that it will continue to mystify a good many would-be commentators until the day when a very great musician will employ his own creative genius to elucidate it, just as Barraqué is now elucidating Debussy. In the meanwhile, generations of pianists will have devoted their efforts to mastering first the technical, then the interpretive problems that it raises. For this music lies outside the scope of our era, in any case; it can belong only to the future.

In this sense, Thomas Mann lacked audacity; in his concern for plausibility he dared not imagine that a twenty-four-year-old composer could outstrip all of contemporary music in a single stride, nor above all, that a man so young could produce music as brilliant and as rigorous—I say this advisedly—as the last works of Beethoven. No music of this density has been composed since *The Great Fugue*, the only ancestor worthy of this unique score; that fact alone should suggest the kind of shock it can produce at first hearing.

Most amazing of all, though, is the fact that this Piano Sonata, which in a sense might seem to have put an end to musical history once and for all, was not its creator's last word; it is incredible that anything could still emerge from the huge sea of silence which engulfed the last, solitary, *absolutely hopeless* notes of that flawless block of music, incredible that anything should emerge to revive the creative impulse and prevent that silence from becoming definitive. True, Barraqué did stop composing for several years (this retirement was interrupted only by his experience with "music for tape"). I myself can testify to the fact that at that time he was entirely unaware of the greatness of his past work and had absolutely no idea of the gigantic enterprise he was about to undertake.

Étude: *"Music for Tape"*

The *Étude* done in the *Musique Concrète* studios appears as a breathing space in Barraqué's career, of which we have as yet seen only the first stage. It is preceded by the works just discussed and followed by the first pages of a work so monumental in its dimensions as to overshadow anything ever conceived in the past. Between them stands this little piece, put together with makeshift materials—"prepared piano" notes distorted with filters—but which nonetheless bears that unmistakable Barraqué stamp. The *Étude* is, of course, a far cry from the aural splendors of Stockhausen's sumptuous compositions done in the Cologne studios. Nor can the now outmoded three-track stereophonic installations of the French Radio's *Club d'Essai* be compared with the setup Edgar Varèse had at his disposal at the Brussels World's Fair. Obviously, the interest of Barraqué's experiment lies elsewhere.

Here, for the first time, he came to grips with the problems involved in absolutely irrational rhythmic patterns; these, as we have already seen,[10] can be fully developed only within the framework of "music for tape." For, although the rhythmic idioms of *Séquence* and the Piano Sonata were highly complex, they were based upon a continuity of tempo, which frequent *accelerandi* and *ritardandi* merely made more flexible. They were essentially *instrumental* idioms, and although their rhythmic structures contained a great many irrational note-values, they still expressed only one tempo at a time. In his *Étude*, Barraqué went a good deal farther; its first few minutes, in particular, display a rhythmic inventiveness which is all the more impressive as it involves extremely long time-values, generally considered rather unwieldy. Moreover, the variation concept that was at the core of his previous works is associated here with a stereophonic "deep-focus" effect which, unfortunately, is only barely perceptible in the commercial recording. Lastly, though some of the "sound-objects" used are not entirely satisfactory—in this sense the *Étude* remains an experimental work—others involve highly subtle tone-color mixtures, and their unprecedented perfection amply justifies Barraqué's purely empirical approach during those months of experimentation.

The opinions expressed by listeners sensitive to Barraqué's music, though often contradictory, generally concur in one respect: all agree that, from beginning to end, his music weaves a fascinating spell to which it is difficult not to succumb. This spell is sustained throughout the five-minute *Étude*, as it is for the eighteen minutes of *Séquence* and, to an even greater degree—but as yet only for "the happy few"—from beginning

---

[10] See Fig. 16 (Chapter Seven).

to end of the Sonata. Each of these works "stands on its own"; it is thoroughly *composed*.

Barraqué is a composer in the highest sense of the word, and seems to have a natural aversion for spectacular, superficial solutions; his are always generated *within* and, as it were, *by* the work itself. This may be why he claims—here I disagree with him—to be "a composer of the past." True, this authentic descendant of Beethoven has not invented a new musical vocabulary, no more than did the composer of the Ninth Symphony. Far from striving to coin musical neologisms, he readily employs the inventions of his predecessors. His tools are almost always traditional: his orchestrations call for only the usual instruments and he always uses the brass in groups; he is partial to the piano and the human voice, accepts the vibraphone but rejects the Ondes Martenot, and uses the various percussion instruments he discovered in Latin American dance bands. Formally speaking, Barraqué is like Debussy in that he refuses to apply any preconceived form to his music; he prefers to let it invent itself as it goes along, finding its own way with each new measure.

Still, I feel that his serial conception, as expressed in his first works, constitutes an original reappraisal of the space-time duality which is at the heart of music. For Barraqué the primordial factor is the interval; of next importance is the note. Every note is dependent upon its situation with respect to the row, for it is linked to and derives from an interval; but aside from this purely dodecaphonic function, it has other functional potentialities. Each note has its own self-contained density, and in the course of a work it should be possible, in one way or another, to "particularize" any given note (by its relative intensity or duration, by assigning it to a given register, by its instrumental situation, or even by deliberately leaving it out of a structure to which it would normally belong). Even on the purely dodecaphonic level, the relationship of note to interval involves problems which may, at any time, call into question the serial concept *per se.* "In order to counteract the uniformity of the melismas arising from the exposition of the row," says Barraqué, "it must be split up continually into sub-groups of three, four, or five notes which undergo various inner permutations." This idea, probably first applied by Berg—in the *Allegro Misterioso* of his Lyric Suite—has been taken up by Barraqué in an "athematical" perspective which obeys the two other modern imperatives of pure variation[11] and discontinuity. Lastly, his block sonorities, grouping several superposed intervals, are, and I quote Barraqué, "a coagulation of space and time which results in a state of neutrality. The sliding, superposed layers that form the Sonata pile up until the very end of the work like so much silt. In *Séquence* they (the block sonorities) stand erect in the middle of the work, a product of the fusion of two rows, and act as a kind of plaster-work around the structure as a whole."

Intervals, notes, and block sonorities are merely the driving forces in a form of perpetual exchange in which time and space proclaim their coexistence and perhaps even their basic identity. It is through this inexhaustible dialectic, in which all elements interact, that the meaning of a given musical "happening" is defined in terms of concomitance or succession.[12] Whether tone-color determines rhythm or vice-versa, whether dynamics depends upon the exposition of the row or vice-versa, all might be regarded as the natural phenomena of a world in which a given note holds several different meanings and in

---

[11] Not, as with Berg, in application of a principle of variations on a single theme.

[12] "Thus," says Barraqué, "if we select, in a row, a sequence of four notes (say A, F, B, G-flat) they will have a spatial reality by virtue of their height or depth, but only a rhythmic decision can organize them in time, and only an orchestral decision can bunch them together or spread them out according to the imperative contingency of constantly evolving form. Simple though it may seem, this phenomenon ultimately leads to a many-dimensional aural apprehension and can therefore set in motion the mechanism of increasing complexity which is nevertheless constantly reversible."

which the work as a whole is the result of an open but limited choice. Such a conception precludes the idea of any single musical parameter's existing prior to another, for here music may be defined as the art of perfect synthesis.

La Mort de Virgile

It remains for me to deal with *La Mort de Virgile*. I cannot pass over in silence a project with which Barraqué has identified himself ever since its conception. On the other hand, however, it would be unseemly to venture the slightest commentary on a work of which only a tiny portion has been written (a portion which, moreover, has not yet been made public). I shall confine myself to a few particulars concerning the work's origins. It is intended to assume vast dimensions, should in fact be much longer than *The Saint Matthew Passion* and *Parsifal* combined. According to the original plan, it will comprise five books. I might add that Book II, which the composer is working on at the present time, is sub-divided into thirteen parts, some of which are grouped in contrasting pairs of *correlatives*.[13] Barraqué intends to use soloists, vocal ensembles, choirs, chamber groups, and several full orchestras, as well as "music for tape" and stereophonic sound.

In 1955, through his friend, the philosopher Michel Foucault, Barraqué became acquainted with Hermann Broch's *The Death of Virgil*, which had just appeared in a French translation. The book fascinated Barraqué; its lyrical and epic tone seemed to him to correspond to the tone of his own music; then, too, the book deals with the creative experience, in other words with Barraqué's own. Broch himself has defined his work in terms which shall one day be famous: "Something absolutely new has

---

[13] Thus, Part III—*le Temps Restitué*—is *correlative* with Part II, *Affranchi de Hasard*. Barraqué prefers this term to *commentary*, a word which he reserves for marginal works that are linked to the central work by allusions and reminiscences but remain distinct from it. ... *Au-dela du Hasard* was presented to the public as a First Commentary on *Affranchi de Hasard* and *Temps Restitué*.

been attempted here; it might be described as a *lyrical commentary on the self.*" No one who is acquainted with Jean Barraqué will find it strange that the great composer should have said to himself: "Broch wrote *The Death of Virgil* for me." In the last analysis, all of Barraqué's music is a "lyrical commentary on the self." As the eminent critic Maurice Blanchot wrote of Broch's novel: "*The Death of Virgil* is the answer. . . . Not that this book actually provides the key to unity, rather is it an image of unity in itself. For Broch there is more at stake in this work than the work itself; if he succeeds in writing it and thereby in reaching that central point wherein the end and the beginning meet, then unity is possible. . . ."[14]

With its starts and stops, its sudden breaks, its irrepressible flights into silence, Barraqué's music thrives on this same temptation of the absolute; like the most lovely passages in Broch's novel, it may be defined, in the composer's own words, as an *oneiric mechanism.*[15] We should bear this phrase in mind,

---

[14] Maurice Blanchot, *Le Livre à Venir*, p. 148, Paris, 1960.

[15] This dream-like phenomenon is probably even more apparent in Barraqué's recent work, ...*Au-dela du Hasard*, which, as I have already pointed out, is related to *La Mort de Virgile*. The piece is shot through with quotations—or rather "reminiscences." In it the music of *La Mort de Virgile* obscurely strives to find itself again, as though in a dream, without ever quite succeeding. The traditional notions of development, gradation, "middle," and "ending" are not applicable here; the work does not even have a real beginning and in the composer's own words, its progression seems "lurching" and "chaotic" (these romantic clichés must of course be interpreted as references to his method of discontinuous musical thought). We are dealing, it seems, with a new—and very strange—conception of form; through a system of "proliferating rows" designed to do away completely with the phenomenon of serial modality, still perceptible in *Séquence*, not only does this work reject every form of recapitulation, but does not even exploit its own attainments as it goes along.

The structure of ...*Au-dela du Hasard* is deliberately heterogeneous, and its aural texture is equally incongruous. The orchestration establishes a contrast between the timbres of modern jazz and those of traditional voices and instruments; a solo part

for in the works of Barraqué, music may well have attained the world of utter strangeness that was partly glimpsed by Beethoven in his last Quartets, by Debussy in *La Mer*, and by Berg in *Wozzeck*; a world in which musical form as such remains en-

---

was specially written for the jazz clarinetist Hubert Rostaing, but the score also called for three other clarinet parts to be played in a perfectly "classical" style. The vocal writing is as flamboyant as that of *Séquence*; it also rests on a similar approach to prosody, but within a far richer phonetic framework. Through a strangely oblique and discontinuous use of the poetic text, Barraqué has managed to achieve an unprecedented blend of words and music. Certain syllables, handled in function of their specific phonetic properties, are combined "harmonically" with other assonant syllables taken from other words sung elsewhere in the score. This, I feel, is a decisive step towards the perfect integration of spoken language into polyphony.

On this level, the work may be said to depart from the heterogeneity which sustains it on other levels. Considering the scope of the enterprise, it is not surprising that the composer should have chosen to write his own text. Divided into seven cantos, it revolves about a quotation from Broch ("Blinded by dreams, and made lucid by dreams . . ."). Musically speaking, the work is composed of thirteen different parts, played without a pause, and lasts just over half an hour. The discontinuous—and at times "diagonal"—enunciation of the text is punctuated by strong interjections. The first nine parts, and especially the ninth (silence-sound-silence, a reminiscence of *Temps Restitué*) are preparatory prefigurations of the tenth; it is in this part that the Broch quotation appears, the center of balance of a work in which everything else is calculated imbalance. Normally, one would expect the work proper to begin here, going on to develop along "harmonious" lines, but actually it is the contrary which occurs; after a few tentative efforts, the score comes to a "spasmodic and disorderly" close, with a panting gasp of exhaustion.

There is much to be said of this work's polyphonic texture, which constitutes a further extension of the concept of a "functional" orchestra inaugurated in *Séquence*. For the next few performances, however, it is probably the work's dramatic power that will attract the greatest interest. For it may turn out that this is the modern form of the music-drama, a *drame-poéme* without plot or characters, which may be the only acceptable replacement for the great, vanished art of opera, last embodied in *Pélléas* and *Wozzeck*.

tirely submerged in the music, defying any attempt at analysis. This may well be the ultimate destiny of the musical work: a dialectical play of memory and presentiment which is impossible to analyze and through which the sense of unity will be at long last incorporated into the "discontinuous continuity" and allusive ambiguities of dreams.

By now the attentive reader may have begun to understand the motives which prompted the deliberately limited selection of composers discussed in this book. As one studies the careers of these eight men, a particular image of contemporary music gradually takes shape; were I to add a ninth this image would not be any clearer, merely less rigorous. Eight great composers in fifty years; perhaps even this list is too long. One wonders how many have infused into their work that secret vitality necessary to ensure its lasting fame. Several of them may already be doomed to be no more than names in a dictionary two hundred years hence, musicological curiosities, revived briefly from time to time.

A particular image of modern music does not, however, mean a biased one. True, five of the masters dealt with here were twelve-tone composers and the other three have, to varying degrees, been attracted to row composition. But this is simply an historical observation. The fact that I have shown a preference for their non-dodecaphonic music—this applies to Berg and Schönberg, as well—should suffice to prove that my choice was not motivated by any hidden sectarianism. Nor was it dictated by some sort of outmoded chauvinism, even though three of the men on my list are Frenchmen and a fourth spent a good many years in France. I hope to have avoided the pitfalls of eclecticism, but I also think I have been pretty severe with a certain kind of "*musique française*"; unlike Jean Cocteau I have spared neither the Cock nor the Harlequin.

In dealing with well-known composers, one has to guard against two equally reprehensible attitudes: indiscriminate admiration and systematic debunking. It is the first that led their contemporaries to consider Rossini greater than Schubert, Meyerbeer greater than Berlioz, and Tchaikovsky greater than Mussorgsky. Transposed into present-day terms, this error is more frequent now than ever before. The second can be useful in destroying false idols, but it fosters an iconoclasm which can be costly indeed! Weber's *Oberon* Overture and Beethoven's Seventh Symphony are liable to be dismissed with the same wave of the hand. I may have found it easier than other critics to avoid errors of this sort. "Between technicians," writes Pierre Boulez, "bluffing is scarcely feasible; no fool's bargain can compensate the observer's frustrations and disappointments."[1] My primary criterion, therefore, was one of technical excellence; this standard allows for no compromise, and it served to delete a good many famous names. Indeed, how can one respect an artist who is not rigorous enough to have carried to its logical conclusion his exploration of the idiom in which he expresses himself, when only by mastering *all* the possibilities of that idiom can he hope to acquire a perfect technique? Certain so-called masterpieces of contemporary music are technically on a level with the Unfinished Symphony, but Schubert's ineffable purity is forever lost to them and nothing can save them from oblivion.

I was mainly concerned, however, with the poetic intensity of a composer's work. Here again Milhaud proved less authentic than Webern and Boulez far more significant than Honegger, while the forlorn little worlds of Britten, Menotti, and their kind simply cannot hold a candle to Barraqué's splendid, shining universe. That poetic criteria should lead to the same conclusions as technical ones comes as no surprise to me. Art thrives on just such correlations, and it is doubtful whether another Schubert—who was, at all events, an exceptional case—could exist in an age when musical language has reached a degree of complexity verging on the impossible.

In the last analysis, I feel that the correct approach to a piece of music can be summed

---

[1] Cf. "Probabilitiés Critiques du Compositeur" in *Domaine Musical*, 1954.

up as a demand for absolute rigor, above and beyond any technical considerations. Just as I am firmly opposed to any form of imitation Gothic or "modernized" Greek architecture, so also do I inveigh loudly against the watered-down musical conceptions foisted on the public as "modern" by most of the recognized music festivals. The works deriving from these conceptions all suffer from a basic want of balance; none of them springs from a vital, fruitful relationship between musical language and form. They recall nothing so much as those hideous New York skyscrapers which try to compensate for the dull bareness of their lower stories with Byzantine, Baroque, or Renaissance spires.

Those works which are outwardly most respectful of tradition infallibly betray that very tradition by their slavish imitation of the tried and true. Like the heir to a once prosperous family who hasn't the courage to change his way of life and loses his fortune by trying to save it, so the neoclassical composer, though he may, at times, gain public approval by catering to its laziness, is doomed to oblivion by two basic failings. The first is his inability to grasp the fact that every new attainment must be paid for by the destruction of an old one; the second, implicit in the first, is his timorous respect for the set forms evolved in the masterpieces of "great historical periods." The neoclassical composer is first cousin to those intellectuals who look upon Culture as an established entity and Beauty as the result of a system of references derived from the mechanical application of traditional values. My reply to this attitude, which automatically excludes from the modern world those who proclaim it, is that the need for transcending itself is an integral part of every genuine culture. Seen in this light, the real descendant of the great masters of the past is the artist who, taking stock of his own powers, feels strong enough to discard the relics of a dead language and sets about recreating the stuff that masterpieces are made of. There has been only one great twentieth-century disciple of Beethoven, and his name is Jean Barraqué, not Vincent d'Indy.

Indeed, since the death of Beethoven, European composers have often tried to recover a sense of classical equilibrium in music; the works of Brahms and Saint-Saëns, though hardly of comparable worth, both attest to this. But what form could an authentic twentieth-century classicism possibly take? Its affiliation with eighteenth-century classicism can be no more than spiritual. Nor can it bear any relationship to the formally imitative and superficially colorful music made fashionable by some of the more brilliant composers of the twenties and thirties. The reply given by Prokofiev's son to a question about his father's working methods is relevant here: "He starts by writing a piece of music that sounds like everyone else's, then he puts the Prokofiev stamp on it." This anecdote greatly oversimplifies the problem, of course, but it does contain a grain of truth. A few displaced accents or a daub of polytonal harmony has often provided a "modern" veneer for works which, left unvarnished, would quite rightly have been deemed completely academic. Obviously, no classicism, in the fullest sense of the term, can be built on this basis. In order to found a new classicism, composers must first elaborate their own forms and language; only then can they create a respectable form of human creation, one which may, indeed, be the goal now being sought—though with completely inadequate methods—by the so-called progressive composers. These, however, are plainly Utopian conjectures. For the present, the critic's task is a more modest one; he must ruthlessly destroy, wherever he finds it growing, that canker of our time, neoclassicism.

CHAPTER NINE

Conclusion

A number of key words and phrases have cropped up repeatedly in the course of the foregoing pages. I have often referred to the "confusion" that prevails in this period of ours which marks the "end of a civilization." Though to some these may seem purely intellectual conceptions, I find the facts themselves rather disturbing. As we have seen, some of the greatest composers of our time completely reversed directions toward the end of their careers. The examples of Schönberg and Stravinsky have taught us that even the noblest creator can lack insight to the point of implicitly repudiating his greatest achievements. And they are not isolated examples: Berg, Bartók, and Prokofiev were just as uncertain and inconsistent in their orientations. This is probably just another sign of the strange times in which we live.

One thing, however, does seem certain: we of the twentieth century will have witnessed the disappearance of the great art of tonal music. The music which has probably constituted the loftiest expression of Western thought from the Renaissance to the present day is now simply falling apart at the seams. The sole ambition of every contemporary composer has been to find his way out of the musical world created by his fore-bears. This common struggle has given rise to a great variety of solutions: "extended" tonality, "loose" tonality, polytonality, a revival of medieval and ancient modes, the use of non-European modes, the invention of new modes, or the total elimination of tonality. This profusion of methods is in itself an element of decomposition. But this interior evidence is corroborated by equally apparent outward signs: the musical situation in our twentieth century is characterized by a revival of academicism, a nostalgic return to the past, a tolerance for amateurism, and the practice of borrowing from non-European traditions.

Of course, our century does not have a monopoly on academic music. There have always been second-rate composers, unable to break away from the past, who have done nothing but re-hash the music of their predecessors. There is every reason to fear that this glorious tradition is still very much alive; the multitude of composers who model their works after music which ought to be no more than a guide-post for them seems to be increasing daily. But there are others, less naïve, who dissemble their academicism in subtle forms which may disconcert the unwary listener. These are the composers who are clever enough to disguise the forms of the past in such startling fashion as to create the illusion of modernity. Charlatans of this ilk—some of whom are not entirely insincere, for they are taken in by their own game—can be compared with people who would like to travel back in time. The two nostalgic attitudes are quite similar, though the latter has at least the merit of self-awareness. The "return to such-and-such" is typical of the twentieth century, and when favored by composers who have given ample proof of their creative powers, it should suffice to show that the tonal world is dying. This "looking backward" does not seem to me a token of allegiance to our great traditions, far from it. It is, on the contrary, an unmistakable symptom of the contemporary composer's waning faith in the future of an organic system whose vital strength is spent.

Amateurism has also assumed a dangerously specious form in our time. Techniques of composition have become so complex that only a very few professional musicians can really master them. Institutionalized musical training is proving more and more inadequate as it lags farther and farther behind the actual state of musical techniques. Paradoxically enough, an increasing number of amateur composers are coming to the fore, due to the ignorance of the public and of certain critics. Faking is now possible and composers lacking the most elementary grasp of musical technique have acquired world-wide reputations. This sort of thing is not, as one might imagine, confined to those forms of musical "entertainment" which delighted the aesthetes of the twenties and thirties. The most complex musical forms are now being tackled by intellectuals who, through the use of highly simplified techniques, easily pass as real composers. Many of these people use the twelve-note row, in particular, as a blind man uses his cane. It has thus become possible to be hailed as a great composer in the twentieth century without even having a sense of pitch.

The practice of borrowing elements from non-European music further confirms the distintegrated state of a musical language whose basic characteristics were purely European in origin. Earlier in this book I have referred to certain elements borrowed from jazz, but merely in order to criticize this practice; I feel that I have adequately demonstrated elsewhere that such a transference is impossible. Many composers, however, feel the need to borrow material, and the results can, under the direction of a more lucid intellect, be musically less gratuitous. Stravinsky's genius enabled him to alter African drum-beats in such a way as to make excellent use of them in one of the loveliest passages of *The Rite of Spring*. But the fact remains that, when introduced into European polyphony, elements from African or Far Eastern music tend to act as dissolving agents. The adoption of such elements by Western composers can, in any case, provide only a temporary solution to the problems raised by the future of tonal music.

One last observation, probably the most important of all, remains to be made. If tonal music is to survive, then tonal composers must develop an entirely new approach, not only to melody and harmony, but—and this, I believe, is essential—to form as well. At one time the achievements of Debussy gave reason to hope that a regeneration of European music through the use of modes had become possible; some still believe this to be true. It is now clear, however, that the great French master's influence on form was ultimately even more destructive than Schönberg's. For nearly a century, now, no new forms have been created within the framework of tonal music; the formal innovations of the leading twentieth-century composers have all tended to transcend the tonal order. Any composer who shrinks from drawing the logical conclusions from this observation necessarily loses all touch with contemporary reality, and is condemned to a life of creative futility and even sterility.

Must we then conclude that our culture is dead? Was Arthur Honegger right in saying that "we are losing our arts"? Are we heading for barbarousness, or will our waning civilization be replaced, on the contrary, by descendants who will be worthy of the past in every respect? Present-day musical development can as yet only begin to provide answers to these questions. It is interesting, however, to examine the meaning of musical composition in those two great nations which, since 1945, have dominated the world and seem to hold the key to the future: the United States and the Soviet Union.

Soviet Music

Soviet music constitutes a problem. One cannot examine it fairly without putting aside one's own political opinions; complete objectivity is indispensable in dealing with a political and social phenomenon as complicated as the context of Russian art today. Objectivity, however, must not be used as an alibi to avoid passing judgment on the actual works produced, nor must it prevent our taking a stand on certain extra-musical factors which do exert an influence on music.

My opinion of Soviet music may seem rather severe, but it is, I think, justifiably so in view of Soviet spokesmen's claim that Russian composers, despite their "errors," are the only true artists of our day. Anyone who sets himself up as "King of the Mountain" is in a very vulnerable position. It may, of course, be objected that most Soviet composers are little more than names to us. This is quite true, and I shall therefore limit my individual judgments to the two leading and least controversial figures, and refrain, for the moment, from expressing my opinion of composers who have not yet been brought to the fore by official Soviet criticism.

At first glance, Soviet music might seem to find a justification in some such adage as "New societies need new art forms," the truth of which would now be generally accepted. If this were the case, if it were possible to distinguish in the works of the major Soviet composers the seeds of a musical conception in keeping with some new type of humanity produced by a new form of society, I would readily excuse any weaknesses, failings, or hesitancies, as I did when dealing with the music of Webern. But to detect any such promise in the Soviet music of recent years—or in what we Westerners have been able to hear of it—requires a far more fertile imagination than mine.

Soviet composers seem to apply in their work a purely utilitarian conception of music. Their attitude can be summed up as follows: music must "also serve"; the composer's role is to glorify the great New Russia, extol the beauty of the workingman's efforts, depict the country's agricultural and industrial development, and express the people's joy and faith in the future of socialism. Needless to say, this requires the composer to remain in constant touch with the masses; otherwise, he will be branded as ineffectual and his works thereby declared null and void. Now mankind's greatest achievements are the work of a minority, whose existence was acknowledged as necessary by the great French socialist, Jean Jaurés (in *La Réalité du Monde Sensible*). These achievements were made possible only by the constant estrangement of this creative minority from the masses. The only way in which the artist can serve his fellow men is by creating works which are almost always beyond the grasp of his immediate contemporaries but which will provide spiritual nourishment for his posterity. The Soviet composer, forced to give priority to his audience—an audience which should be as large as possible as soon as possible—has no alternative but to write anachronistic music, more or less cleverly disguised in a cloak of "modernism." His chief concern is no longer to "divine the future and aspire to be part of it," as Wagner so admirably phrased it, but merely to avoid disturbing his contemporaries in their listening habits. This subordination of the creative artist to purely social contingencies actually results in the negation of the very notion of progress upon which these contingencies are predicated. "Socialist realism," which was adopted, after a brief period of uncertainty, as the official doctrine of Soviet art, can hardly be considered, in the light of the works it has fostered, as anything better than a modern form of the most reactionary, academic conventionalism. It would be astonishing were any artistic creation worthy of the name to develop in the U.S.S.R. so long as its rulers fail to realize their mistake.

If one tends to blame the present state of affairs on persons other than the composers themselves, this is because Soviet music does appear to be so closely controlled from above. The officially accepted composer probably enjoys a higher status in the Soviet social hierarchy than in any other country in the world. But there are very strict obligations attached to this privileged position. The composer is no longer sole judge of the direction his music is to take. Struggles of an essentially intimate nature are fought out in public. Official committees are appointed to supervise the way in which the masters of Soviet music conceive their work, and they may find "unprogressive" tendencies in the music of leading composers. "Bourgeois formalism" is a cardinal sin to these modern inquisitors who, in all probability, understand nothing of contemporary developments in music. Composers like Shostakovich and even Prokofiev must consequently acknowledge their "errors" and let men who, musically speaking, would hardly deserve to be their pupils, interfere with the working of their creative processes and alter their orientations. That anyone should claim to know better than the artist himself what path he should follow, that an outsider should be able to send him down a path which was not of his own choosing—no matter what path he might choose if left to himself—seems to me a shocking infringement of the critic upon the artist's domain.

I am aware of having simplified the problems raised by Soviet music. Government policy in this matter has not always been what it is today. In Lenin's time, the government's liberal policy allowed for doctrines which were resolutely "modern" (though in the bad sense of the term). Open conflicts between composers of conflicting tendencies later arose until, at the end of the second World War, the order was given to avoid Western influences at all costs. There have been signs of a change since Stalin's death, though it is still hard to tell how far-reaching it will be. Will the Russian leaders go so far as to reconsider the very premises of Soviet music? In actual fact, the problem can only be resolved when moral considerations cease to enter into art, when a Metternich grants to some future Beethoven the right to express himself as he sees fit.

Immediately after the war, similar tendencies began to appear in the People's Democracies. A few months after Zhdanov had proclaimed from Moscow that Soviet composers must write music of a "national" character, "healthily optimistic" as against the "cosmopolitan, individualistic morbidity" of bourgeois art, a group of composers from the Cominform countries met in Prague and drafted a program for what they called "progressive" music. There is no doubt but what this doctrine—actually rather vague, as it consists of nothing but moral precepts—now constitutes the official line in music and that those who depart from it must have a pretty hard time making themselves heard.

Sergei Prokofiev, born in 1891, was, until his death in 1953, one of the major figures in Soviet music, even though he lived abroad during the first fifteen years of the new régime. He was an extremely gifted composer, but his career is a perfect example of what can happen when an artist falls prey to the confusion of our transitional period. His reaction against the subtle impressionism in vogue at the turn of the century expressed itself in three successive manners. In his early works it took the form of a rather gratuitous aggressiveness, with extravagant harmonies and simplistically brutal rhythms. In the twenties, he passed into a "neoclassical" phase, of which the fortunately ironic *Classical Symphony* may be considered an earlier forerunner. Finally, his adherence to official Soviet doctrine led him into conventional, academic paths with such elaborate pieces of bombast as *Alexander Nevsky*. Though he underwent the most conflicting influences—echoes of *The Rite of Spring* turn up in *Ala and Lolly* (*The Scythian Suite*), parts of *Chout* were inspired by *Les Noces*, and the ideas of Les Six became more and more apparent in his music after World War I—Prokofiev did have a character all his own, and his best works reveal a very personal sensibility. His prolific output can probably be explained in terms of the often over-simplified nature of the music he wrote. But while he had little sense of form, he did have a flair—a rather anachronistic one, it is true—for melody. His orchestrations often display his solid craftsmanship, acutely sensitive ear, and unerring sense of poetic effect; in a few works, such as *Ala and Lolly*, the orchestration is sumptuous. It is a pity that a composer of Prokofiev's gifts never acquired a better understanding of the problems raised by new developments in music. His most successful writing can probably be found in what would appear to be his least ambitious scores; *Peter and the Wolf*, for example, is undeniably a masterpiece of light classical music, a field in which precious few composers have written well, though a great many have tried their hand at it.

Dmitri Shostakovich (born in Saint Petersburg in 1906) has, since the death of Prokofiev, generally been considered the leading figure in Soviet music. He began his studies under Glazunov at the Petersburg conservatory, and became famous in 1925 with his First Symphony, op. 10. Among his best known works are the *October Symphony* (1927), the *Leningrad Symphony*, written during the siege of that city, *The Song of the Forest*, an oratorio, an opera called *The Nose*, and the ballet *Bright Rivulet*. This last-named work, together with his opera *Lady Macbeth of Mzensk*, was officially criticized by the Union of Soviet Composers, who took Shostakovich to task for writing in a "formalist" and "insincere" idiom. The works under attack would have been considered perfectly harmless in the West, but they contained a few "daring" passages which, though actually quite timid and of doubtful significance, were nevertheless too strong. Shostakovich had to cleave to the line once more, and the sub-title of his Fifth Symphony is perfectly explicit: "A Soviet Artist's Reply to Justified Criticisms."

Shostakovich's abundant output is extremely uneven. As a composer, he may, in some respects, be compared with Honegger: he has the same forcefulness and, at times, the same sense of grandeur, but then nothing is more dangerous than biting off more than one can chew. I cannot, of course, know what Shostakovich's real intentions were in composing a work like *The Song of the Forest,* but judging it on its merits alone, one is forced to conclude that this score, which reaches new heights in phony lyricism and grandiloquence, and which often sounds like an imitation of Borodin, is dreadfully feeble. Shostakovich is a much less subtle musician than Prokofiev, and his mistake is to be so much more ambitious.

I doubt that greater freedom would have saved Shostakovich's music from mediocrity. His fate, therefore—not to mention those of Kabalevsky or Khachaturian—seems hardly worth discussing. One point, however, does remain obscure. We do know that there exist in the Soviet Union and the People's Democracies composers who have had no official recognition. I know nothing of their work, I do not even know their names. Just how interesting is their music? What kind of audience have they? Are they able to have their works performed at all? Can it be that, despite forty years of cultural isolation, they are writing music which is in step with the major innovations of our time? Or are they, on the contrary, merely latter-day disciples of Schönberg? Time will tell whether the composers of today, sacrificed in one way or another on the altar of posterity, will not have been sacrificed in vain. The fact remains that, for the present, official Russian music is on a par with the battle paintings of the Napoleonic era.

American Music

The situation of music in the United States is entirely different from what it is in the U.S.S.R. In America, the freedom of expression is so great that one would have expected it to produce a vast creative movement. The reasons for the American composer's lack of interest in the most vitally active tendencies of European music are difficult to determine. He has never been kept in ignorance of what was going on abroad. He was always free to observe the progress of the new musical language and to judge it as he saw fit. He was at liberty to adopt it or even to contribute to its development, if he so wished, unhampered by the interference of a Zhdanov. Moreover, in America, the powers that be take an active interest in culture. Wealthy, powerful foundations subsidize organizations whose avowed aim is the propagation of modern music. And yet this is the Western country which has given Shostakovich's music its warmest welcome, and which buys more records of Prokofiev than of Berg, Webern, and Schönberg put together. How is it that Soviet academicism is so popular with the American public?

It may seem unfair to link the state of music in America with the taste of its public. After all, in many ways the American concert-goer resembles the mass of French music lovers who applaud those so-called great composers who rose to fame between the first and second World Wars. In France, however, a few individuals have reacted violently against this standardization, and expressed their protest in the form of music, first in the works of Messiaen, and later in those of Boulez and Barraqué. Thus, France has saved herself, as she occasionally does, from her mediocre offspring by giving birth to a few exceptional artists. Unfortunately, nothing of the kind has occurred in the United States to make up for the public's lack of discrimination. One looks in vain for a genius—or even a really gifted composer—in the history of American music; the important figures are all European born. The only major composers of whom American music can boast acquired American citizenship long after their music had fully matured and when it was already on the decline. It is a credit to the United States to have given asylum to composers who were denied the right to create—and in some cases the right even to remain alive— in the countries of their birth. One might suppose that such composers could not fail, as teachers and as living examples, to stimulate creative activities which would, sooner or later, have unpredictable results. On the contrary, however, American composers generally ignored the most interesting aspects of their contributions and heeded only the most questionable. Sad to say, they seem to have followed the baleful examples set by Stravinsky after 1930, and by Paul Hindemith.

The name of Hindemith—whose prolific output was banned in Nazi Germany—has, to my mind, acquired a symbolic meaning. He has tried his hand at every kind of composition, from the rather heavy-handed buffoonery of an opera like *Neues vom Tage* to the sublimity he sought to attain through the use of the major classical forms. His neoclassicism is, however, less conscious and deliberate than Stravinsky's. Though he, too, like the composer of *The Rite of Spring,* ultimately "returned to Bach," with Hindemith it was not so much through a conscious *volte-face* as through an almost natural inclination. In this respect, he can be said to have inherited Brahms' tendency for retrogressive development. His series of chamber concertos—called *Kammermusik*—give a fairly good picture of his early development; after the first tentative gropings, he soon withdrew into his shell and refused to face the problems confronting all his contemporaries and resulting from the use of pure chromaticism, the transcending of tonality, and the disintegration of rhythmic patterns. Similarly, he found in the traditional forms the most comfortable molds in which to shape his full-blown lyricism, which is, however, like that of Brahms, tempered by a certain sobriety. Worst of all, in his best-known works—*Mathis der Mahler* and *Nobilissima Visione*—Hindemith seems to achieve his own aesthetic goal. Paul Hindemith's stilted, dismal music has never once attained the realm of authentic beauty. Indifferent to the marvelous inventions of Debussy and to the basic contributions of more recent masters, he is representative of his period only in its most negative aspects. His music lacks faith in the beauty of the new forms. It is a fossilized music whose very existence closes doors on vistas we would like to forget were ever revealed at all.

Now, once we agree that Hindemith's music is a lamentable error, we must go on to dismiss neoclassicism as a whole and, with it, nearly all of American music.

For Piston, Thomson, and Copland have all been schooled in a tradition of decadent Stravinskyism, as taught by the musically short-sighted Nadia Boulanger, who enjoys considerable prestige in the United States and still exerts an unfortunate influence there. Antheil, Barber, Harris, Nabokov, Schumann, and Wolpe are all neoclassicists. So, in their way, are Sessions, Ben Weber, the twelve-tone composers grouped about Milton Babbitt, and most of the newcomers: Carter, Harrison, Helm, Rorem and dozens of others upon whom the music festivals have not yet bestowed official recognition. As far as music is concerned, the choices which have been made in America reveal as academic and traditionalist a climate as that which prevails in the Soviet Union. American music, like Soviet music, claims to be turned towards the future; in reality, both are merely part of an historical process by which the tonal forms of music are irremediably falling into disuse.

It is true, of course, that in the United States composers like Gunther Schuller and Earle Brown can have their works performed. Their music can compete openly with the music of "official composers" for public favor. But, aside from the fact that, until now, their appeal has gone practically unheeded, these men do not seem to have turned out works of overwhelming stature, comparable to those dealt with in this book.[1]

---

[1] I have already examined, in an earlier chapter, the pioneering roles of Edgar Varèse and John Cage, whose uneven works may be considered "transitional achievements," valid only insofar as they are transcended by others (as, indeed, they have been). On the eve of the second World War certain intellectuals, in their eagerness to hail the birth of an authentic American music, had

It is almost as though the American composer suffered from that preoccupation with audience reaction which is, as we have seen, imposed in a less subtle form upon the Soviet composer. True, it does require a mighty faith in one's own creative gifts to follow the path of loneliness and silence, trusting in posterity to right all wrongs. It may be, too, that the symbolic importance of financial success in America tends to discredit in his own eyes the composer to whom recognition is slow in coming. But, be that as it may, whatever one's sympathy for the United States, and no matter how much one may admire a conductor like Mitropoulos, a violinist like Heifetz, or a pianist like David Tudor (who has given such brilliant performances of Boulez, Stockhausen, Pousseur, and Cage) one is forced to conclude that America has not yet produced any music worthy of her architecture or literature. Her one truly creative contribution has been jazz. Beyond that, American music offers no equivalent of the United Nations building, only a succession of Washington Capitols.

---

already built up a legend around Charles Ives. To the French critic, who is constantly having to debunk the apparently indestructible Fauré myth, attacking the Ives myth may seem a bit old hat, but it takes on a completely different meaning in the light of the American musical situation as described above. Ives, however, had a bent for experimentation, and though he was unable to carry it to a successful conclusion, he may be regarded as a remote precursor of Stockhausen.

On the other hand, it would seem that since my last trip to the United States in 1957 things have taken a turn for the better. The American public, I am told, is less oblivious to row music than it used to be, and it seems that a fresh group of young composers is steering away from both neoclassicism and academic dodecaphonism, to strike out for less comfortable horizons. Can it be that a veritable school of young serial musicians is about to change the face of American music? I certainly hope that among these young men—who are still only names to me (Chou Wen Chung, Di Domenica, Huggler, Lombardo, London, Martino, Spies, Subotnik, Westergard, Wyner and others)—there will be at least one whose work will corroborate my criticisms at the same time that it makes them obsolete.

It is not too surprising that a country as young as the United States, or a society which, like the U.S.S.R., has barely emerged from infancy, should have provided the world with no authentic musical masterpieces. If music *is* the art of arts—as I believe it to be—if it *is* the noblest road to beauty, then it can flourish only at the summit of a structure which has been many generations in the making, and which may well testify to that same human suffering which these new societies aim to do away with. The greatness of France and Austria—both countries with glorious pasts, both sorely damaged by war—lies in the fact that they made it possible (Austria in the twenties and thirties, France in the forties and fifties) to transcend the values of a world in which their splendor was so deeply rooted. Hence, that period which witnessed the breakdown of spiritual and cultural values which precedes the fall of any empire or civilization produced the seed of a new, international art form. And although this form was definitely linked to the past, it energetically called into question all the principles which had sustained Western music for centuries.

"The art of arts"; this is not meant to be a figure of speech. It is self-evident to me that the history of music in the West has been a far more extraordinary phenomenon than that of architecture or the visual arts. By temporarily simplifying certain elements such as rhythm, Western polyphonists managed to create an entirely new medium in which the germination of such superior forms of life as Bach's fugues or Beethoven's quartets became possible, and though these works may seem terribly familiar to us now, they are, *when seen in the light of human civilization as a whole, extremely unusual*. These monsters of beauty may, in their multi-dimensional quality, well be the prefigurations of a "superhuman" art, in Nietzsche's sense of the word, which was never even approached by Da Vinci, Rembrandt, or Van Gogh. This may be why they came so late in history; two and a half centuries ago nothing of the sort had so much as been dreamt of. The conception of *The Art of the Fugue* was made possible by the infinite pains of a staggeringly vast number of composers; it marked the end of collective creation in music. Scores like Beethoven's *Hammer-klavier Sonata* and Twelfth Quartet constitute a singular event in the course of human thought, a kind of forward leap—one might almost speak of a mutation—which has never occurred in the history of any other civilization. Indeed, no other civilization can offer any musical equivalents of Japanese classical paintings or pre-Columbian sculpture to compare with the more than exceptional works cited above. Woven thread by thread, as it were, in that absolutely unparalleled process which is *composition*, these works raised artistic creation to a level of artificiality hitherto unknown; they were the earliest manifestations of an aesthetic conception which is fundamentally artificial and abstract, and it is these qualities which have made music the purest and most precious creation of the human soul.

A heritage of this kind is a heavy burden to bear. The greatness of the serial conception is that it assumes all the responsibilities implicit in this heritage. With or without the help of electronic techniques, serial music cannot fail to be even more artificial and abstract than the most artificial and abstract works from which it originally derives, thereby penetrating the human soul more deeply than any previous art form. There is, of course, reason to fear that future composers may simply collapse beneath such a tremendous weight. Even now, the raw materials of music seem to resist the composer's manipulations as they did not in the eighteenth century. For a long time to come, we shall have, almost inevitably, fewer and fewer works of really great stature. A certain kind of great composer—great in the sense that Vivaldi, Mendelssohn, or Verdi were—will cease to exist: in the future more real genius will be required to write a piece of great music. And everything which is less than great will sink to the same level of dull mediocrity; Salieri and Haydn will join hands in their common impotence and regret that neither of them is Mozart. There is real danger that music may actually breed its own death, not through its inability to break away from its traditions, as would have been the case had the neoclassical reaction had its way, but from having set its sights infinitely high. Music, by the very nature of its language, will tend towards absolute purity; those works which fail to attain this purity will be condemned in proportion to their ambitions, and the higher these have been, the harder shall be their fall.

The musical universe implicit in the serial conception is one which no longer allows for any sort of compromise. No longer can another Ravel be tolerated on the grounds of his "lightness"; no "sense of humor" can possibly justify the existence of another Satie; even irony will have lost its reason for being, since it can no longer have any object. The serial work can only be pure music, striving to express the most difficult, hidden beauty. Though it does seem certain that the great composer will be rarer in the future than at any time in the past, the ideal conditions for the emergence of a very great composer—greater perhaps than the most towering geniuses of the past—do exist.

Will this unique creator ever appear? Is he already amongst us? Can he be Jean Barraqué, the young Frenchman whose first, dazzling achievements I have already described? These are momentous questions. In the words of an ancient Chinese text, quoted by Borges: "We might look a unicorn square in the face and not be sure whether it really is a unicorn or not. We know that a certain hairy animal is called a horse, that a certain horned animal is known as a bull, but we do not know what a unicorn looks like." Only the years to come—the years during which Barraqué should continue to compose *La Mort de Virgile*—may provide an answer to this impassioned query, anguish-ridden in its implied doubt as to the ultimate worth of our era. A period which has witnessed so many failures and which is characterized by so much injustice can find redemption in the eyes of History only through a constellation of works as dazzling as those produced by the Florentine *cinquecento*. Posterity may not, however, detect that constellation in the art of our time. Failing that, the only possible redeeming factor would be a single, absolutely unique work, one which sums up and transcends all that man has created through the ages. The mere existence of a work such as this, the possibility that its mighty stream may strike through the veil of fashionable praise (like that which was heaped on *Pelleas*) or of fashionable sneers (like those which greeted Beethoven's last quartets) to spread a few, precious drops across the centuries, reaching, perhaps, the humblest and most beauty-starved of mortals, will mean our era was not exclusively destructive. As Nietzsche put it, the ultimate aim of art is "to make all men artists, to arouse the sleeping genius in the common man."

Glossary

ADDED NOTE   A note which is not properly part of a given chord according to the established rules but which is added to it. Among the most characteristic examples of added notes, Olivier Messiaen cites the augmented fourth and the major sixth (in the major or minor triad).

ADDED VALUE   A short note, a rest, or simply a dot which serves to prolong one of the component values of a rhythmic cell. (Messiaen; see Fig. 11, page 106.)

ANACRUSIS—ACCENT—TERMINATION   These three words sum up the rhythmic aspect of the conflict between tension and repose as it existed in classical music. In Messiaen's music the anacrusis (or preparation for the accent) often assumes enormous proportions, thus foreshadowing the disruption of this notion and the appearance of a new rhythmic conception.

ATHEMATICISM   Musical concept based upon the rejection of the theme as a generating principle, the unity of a given work being established by other means (rigorous handling of the rows, variations on rhythmic cells, etc.).

ATTACK   The manner in which a sound is initially emitted. A diversity of attacks can produce appreciable differences of tone-color, especially on the piano. Messiaen was the first to organize attacks in terms of specific structures.

AUGMENTATION   Consists in extending the duration of the rhythmic values in a given motif. In classical music, augmentation generally consisted in doubling every value (the eighth note became a quarter, and the quarter a half). In contemporary music, augmentation is often asymmetrical (the various values are not all increased in the same ratio).

BLOCK SONORITIES   Fixed, vertical aggregates composed of several structurally related notes.

CADENCE   In classical music: ending of a phrase; also, any harmonic formula meant to express or emphasize this ending.

CANON   In classical music: a species of composition in which two or more parts take up the same subject one after another in strict and continuous imitation, observing the same intervals.

Rhythmic canon: In modern music (Olivier Messiaen): A canon which affects only the note-values of a given fragment, not its melodic intervals. Like the ordinary canon, a rhythmic canon can be combined with the various forms of augmentation or diminution (e.g., canon obtained by dotting notes).

CHROMATICISM   That which is based on a preponderance of chromatic relationships and tends to divide the octave into twelve half tones rather than seven degrees.

Absolute Chromaticism: A system in which diatonicism is completely eliminated from harmony and melody. It results in the abolition of tonal functions and consequently in non-tonality; it is at the origin of *dodecaphonism.*

Total Chromatic: The twelve notes which, in Western music, form the harmonic and melodic vocabulary, considered independently of any hierarchy.

CONJUNCT   Said of a melodic style in which small intervals (especially seconds) are predominant.

CONTRAPUNTAL   Polyphonic writing conceived in the spirit of counterpoint, and which tends to favor the linearity of the different parts. Opposite of *harmonic.*

DEFECTIVE   Said of a mode derived from another, larger mode and contained within it. In this sense, the pentatonic scale (C – D – F – G – A) is a defective form of the ordinary major scale.

DEGREE   In the tonal system: that which results from the diatonic division of the octave. The ordinary major or minor scale is composed of seven degrees, some of which may be said to have precedence over others (the "strong" or "good" degrees are the 1st or tonic, 5th or dominant, and 4th or sub-dominant).

DERIVATIVE ROW   A form of the row whose relationship with the original row is more complex than those which result from its transposition, retrogradation, or inversion. (See Fig. 4, page 62.)

DEVELOPMENT, MAIN and TERMINAL   Two parts of the *sonata form* (see definition).

DIATONICISM   That which results from the diatonic scale, major or minor, with its unevenly spaced degrees (separated, that is, by either a half or a whole tone). Diatonicism implies some sort of hierarchy, either tonal or modal. It is the opposite of *chromaticism.*

DIMINUTION   A technique opposite to that of *augmentation.* Here the values are shortened, either according to a fixed ratio, as in classical music (the quarter note becoming an eighth and so forth), or asymmetrically, as in modern music.

DISCONTINUITY   Said of a polyphonic fabric based on constantly varying rhythmic patterns, a disjunct melodic line, a contrasting succession of tone-colors and frequent breaks in the musical tissue. Opposite of *linearity* (in the modern sense).

DISJUNCT   Said of a melodic style in which large intervals predominate.

DISPLACED RHYTHM OR RHYTHMIC DISPLACEMENT   The shifting of a rhythmic structure with respect to the meter (e.g.: syncopation of an element which was originally unsyncopated).

DODECAPHONISM   Conception tending towards an organization of the melodic and harmonic relationships proceeding from *absolute chromaticism.* Pure dodecaphonism implies the equality— and even the mutual neutrality—of the twelve notes of the total chromatic. (See *Row.*)

DOMINANT   The fifth degree of the major or minor scale in the tonal system. As it is the fundamental of the chord having the closest relation to the tonic chord, this degree plays a predominant role in balancing the tonal functions; the tonic-dominant relationship may be said to sum up the conflict of tension and respose as expressed in classical music.

DYNAMICS   In contemporary music: intensities considered as a whole; the language which results from their systematization.

ELECTRONIC MUSIC   See page 140, note 6.

ELECTROPHONIC   Said of those technical processes used to produce synthetic sound-objects which are preserved on magnetic tape. Electronic music and concrete music are both based upon the use of electrophonic techniques. For a definition of these terms see page 140, note 6.

FORM   Manifestation of the need for unity within a given work; the manner in which a work asserts its unity, overcoming the space-time duality which conditions all polyphonic music (see *Thematicism, Athematicism*).

   Small Form: A type of form in which only a very limited sampling of the possibilities afforded by the work's basic material are actually exploited or which derives from raw material so limited that no extensive development of it is possible. The "small form" engenders works of short duration (Webern's Pieces for String Quartet, Berg's Pieces for Clarinet, etc.).

   Large-Scale Form: Type of form in which the work is fully realized, in which the basic raw material undergoes a series of transformations which may in themselves constitute attainments to be exploited in turn. In contrast with classical large-scale forms, which derived from clearly defined archetypes such as the fugue and the sonata, the large-scale forms of contemporary music stem from the concept of "athematicism" and are of a *fluctuating* nature (constantly evolving forms, "open" forms, etc.).

HALF OR SEMI TONE   The smallest division of the octave in Western music. The "distance" separating each of the twelve notes of the chromatic scale.

HARMONIC (*adj.*)   In polyphony: type of writing in which the vertical grouping of the notes tends to take precedence over the linearity of the individual parts. Opposite of *contrapuntal*.

HARMONIC(s) (*noun*)   Acoustical effect(s) with a characteristic timbre that may be obtained on stringed and wind instruments.

HARMONIC PROGRESSION   Symmetrical reproduction of a harmonic-melodic model on various degrees of the scale.

HOMOPHONIC   Said of polyphonic vocal writing in which all the syllables are uttered simultaneously in each part.

HORIZONTAL   1) Term used to describe all elements written horizontally on a score and which are, therefore, heard successively.

2) In polyphony, *horizontal writing* tends to emphasize the *linearity* of the different parts.

INTENSITY   In contemporary music this term has come to replace the less precise term of dynamics. Changes of intensity, ranging from *pppp* to *ffff* can give rise to specific structures.

INTERVAL   "Distance" separating two notes. An interval is *harmonic* or *vertical* when the two notes are sounded simultaneously; it is *melodic* or *horizontal* when they follow one another.

A melodic interval is either *ascending* or *descending*. When the two component notes lie next to one another in the scale (e.g.: G – A), the interval is said to be *conjunct;* otherwise it is described as *disjunct*.

INVERSION   1) In the harmonic sense: inverting an interval so that the lower note becomes the higher (e.g., the third C–E becomes the sixth E–C).

2) In a broader sense (as used in row music): the "reversing" of a melodic figure in such a way that, while the intervals remain the same, those which were ascending become descending, and vice-versa (e.g., the ascending melodic figure G A C becomes the descending figure G F D).

IRRATIONAL (Time- or Note-) VALUE   Value obtained by dividing a basic value by any number which is not a direct multiple of two (an eighth note in a quintuplet is an irrational value).

Irrational rhythm is a concept based on the intensive use of irrational values; it dispels the impression of metric continuity produced by the binary (or even ternary) division of the beat. Irrational rhythm as such also tends to preclude any meter based on a fundamental time-value.

ISORHYTHM   The application of a given rhythmic pattern to various melodic patterns.

KLANGFARBENMELODIE   Melody of tone-colors. By analogy with the succession of different notes which characterizes melody *per se*, contemporary composers, since Schönberg and Webern, employ a rapid succession of different tone-colors, either for purely expressive purposes, or as an integral part of the work's structure.

LINEARITY   1) In the classical sense: that which is distinctly perceptible as an autonomous element of continuity within the framework of a polyphonic fabric; e.g. the linearity of the various parts in a Bach fugue. Opposite of *verticality*.

2) In the modern sense: the use of a distinct tone-color (or family of tone-colors) which emphasizes a certain uniformity of the rhythmic and melodic structures in the polyphonic fabric. Opposite of *discontinuity*.

"LOOSE" or "EXTENDED" TONALITY   Notions which, though they are still related to the principle of tonal unity, tend to reject the restrictions of classical tonal functions, thereby attenuating that unity.

MELISMA   In modern music: any melodic figure (resulting, for example, from a fragment of a row).

METER   A schematic representation of the rhythmic substructure which exists prior to the rhythmic patterns themselves. Greek meter made use of long and short values; classical meter was based on measures of equal length divided into strong and weak beats.

Un-measured Meter: A conception by which the even divisions of the classical meter tend to be replaced by measures of unequal length, sometimes composed of beats that are uneven, as well, constituting free multiplications of a basic value (Messiaen).

MODAL   In contemporary music this adjective refers to any use in a given work of more than two modes. *Polymodal* refers to the superposition of two or more modes (cf. Fig. 12a, page 108).

MODES   Diatonic or semi-chromatic scales which differ by the number of notes employed as well as by the intervals separating these notes.

Ancient Modes: mainly the Greek and Ecclesiastical modes.

Non-European Modes: mainly Indian and Chinese.

Classical Modes: the major and minor scales of the tonal system.

New Modes: those created in our time (such as Messiaen's modes of limited transposition).

MORPHOLOGY   As first applied to music by Pierre Boulez, it refers to the written texture as well as the "syntax" of a polyphonic work.

MUSIC FOR TAPE   Expression used to describe any work executed by means of electrophonic techniques and conveyed through magnetic tape.

MUSIQUE CONCRETE   See page 140, note 6.

NON-TONAL or ATONAL   Refers to any music having no tonal or modal polarizations, in other words music in which the tonal functions have been suspended. In atonal music, the notes are not organized according to any hierarchy; there is neither tonic nor dominant.

OSSIA   Term by which the composer allows the performer to play a given variant of a passage.

OSTINATO   The "obstinate" repetition of any single pattern, either rhythmic or melodic.

PARAMETERS, or COMPONENTS   Height and depth of notes, tone-color, attacks, intensity, duration, and tempo, as well as their directional source.

PARLANDO   As though spoken. (See *Sprechgesang*.)

PEDAL-POINT   In classical music: a long, held note which constitutes a strong assertion of the key (tonic or dominant pedal-point) and is able even to sustain chords to which it is entirely foreign.

> *Rhythmic pedal-point:* The name Messiaen has given to a form of *ostinato* which, like the rhythmic canon, affects only the values of the notes and not their height or depth. (See Fig. 12a, page 108.)

> *Pedal-point group:* Name given by Messiaen to the repetition within a single part, of a melodic structure which is superposed on independent elements in the other parts.

PERMUTATION   A modification in the usual order of two or more notes in a given row.

POLYPHONY   In the contemporary sense, this word means any music in which two or more musical "happenings" (e.g., different melodic lines or rhythms carried by different parts) may take place simultaneously.

POLYRHYTHM   The superposition of two or more differently constituted rhythmic structures.

POLYTONALITY   Results from the superposition of two or more
melodic fragments (or melodic structures) written in different
keys. Much abuse has been made of this term; it is not to be
confused with *polymodality*, which people often mean when
they speak of polytonality.

QUARTER TONE   Obtained by dividing the octave into twenty-four
equal parts. Used by certain contemporary polyphonists (Haba,
Wichnegradsky, and occasionally Boulez).

RECAPITULATION   In the classical "sonata form": the return of the
first and then the second theme in the original key, following
the main development.

REGISTERS   Sub-divisions of a tessitura: high, medium, and low.
In serial music, one or more notes may, at times, be assigned to
a given register for the duration of a given section.

RETROGRADATION or RETROGRADE MOTION   Presentation of the notes
of a melodic fragment in an order which is the reverse of that
in which they have previously been heard, in other words
from the last note to the first. Reading a melodic or harmonic
succession from right to left. Also known as *crab-form*.

RETROGRADE-INVERSION or INVERTED CRAB-FORM   Combination of
inversion (in the broader sense) with retrograde motion.

ROW or SERIES   1) Twelve-tone row or series: the systematic organization of the twelve notes of the total chromatic, arranged
in an order chosen beforehand by the composer. This *original
row*, its inversion, its retrogradation (crab-form), its retrograde-inversion, as well as their eleven possible transpositions,
go to make up the forty-eight possible forms in which a single
row may be used.

2) Since Boulez, this *serial principle* is commonly applied
to the other components of music: series (or rows) of block
sonorities, time-values, tone-colors, attacks, intensities, etc.,
may be employed simultaneously.

SERIAL   Refers, in this book, to any music making general use of
the generating principle of the series or *row*.

SERIAL MODALITY   Neologism used to designate the impression of
repetition ultimately produced by any relatively long twelve-

tone score, owing to the very limited number of possibilities offered by the forty-eight forms of a given row.

SFORZANDO   Sharp accent.

SONATA FORM   In classical music, this is a piece composed upon two main themes and involving an *exposition* and a main *development* of this thematic material, then a *recapitulation* and, in some cases, a *terminal development*.

SOUND-OBJECT (from the French: *Objet Sonore*)   A complex sound which generally results from the electrophonic treatment of one or more sounds (musical sounds or noises) and which cannot be expressed in terms of any classified sonority. Certain instrumental works of Varèse and Webern, and especially the "prepared piano" works of Cage, contained prefigurations of the sound-object; but this relatively recent development is chiefly due to the techniques of *music for tape*. (See note 6 page 140.)

SPIEGELBILD   Mirror canon. A structural procedure which consists in the retrogradation, starting from a central pivotal point (the mirror) of all the notes played up to that point, from the last to the first. (See Fig. 8, page 77.)

SPRECHGESANG   Spoken melody or inflected speech. Schönberg and Berg used this word to designate a kind of declaimed melody, bordering on speech.

TEMPERAMENT   Accoustical system suggested by Werckmeister in 1691 and worked out by Neidhardt in 1706. It was strongly advocated by Rameau and by Bach (cf. *The Well-Tempered Clavichord*). Temperament is a system for tuning the piano and the organ artificially, by dividing the octave into twelve rigorously equal half tones. It has been adopted in all countries of Western tradition.

TESSITURA   1) The range of notes best suited to a voice or instrument; e.g., the bassoon's tessitura.

2) The average range of notes in which a given score is written: e.g., the low tessitura of the Sixth Brandenberg Concerto.

THEMATICISM   In classical music: a notion based upon the relations between the *theme*—a genetic musical idea, generally melodic—and various extensions of it, such as variations or developments. The classical sonata movement, or "sonata form," with its two themes, is one of the most important thematic forms, and its echo is still to be heard in many modern works.

TONAL   Said of anything and everything pertaining to the world of tonality.

   Tonal functions: roles played by the various degrees and the chords supported by them within the framework of the tonal system.

TONALITY   1) Tonal system. A set of phenomena and structures proceeding from the fact that a privileged note or *tonic* is regarded as the point of reference for all the other notes used. The rules of tonality.

   2) Key. A set of notes which necessarily form one of the classified scales, either major or minor; e.g. the key—or tonality—of F major.

TONAL REMINISCENCE   A phenomenon of so-called tonal polarization, resulting from the consonance of a given note-group, or from its resemblance to a classified chord; the early twelve-tone composers systematically sought to avoid this sort of thing.

TONIC   First degree on the scale of the tonal system. It is this note which gives its name to the key. It is the "most important" note in that key, more important than the dominant.

TRANSPOSITION   Changing the height or depth of a melodic fragment without changing the relationships of its component intervals.

TREMOLANDO   Refers to the *tremolo* effect (rapid fluttering on a single note or, at times, on several alternate notes).

"TRUE" or "NATURAL" HARMONY   That harmonization which most faithfully reflects the harmonic implications of the melody which it is accompanying.

VALUE (Time- or Note-)   Duration of a note, as measured from the moment of its emission.

VARIATION   1) In classical music the theme and variations, for example, is a set form.

   2) As a compositional device it consists in embroidering upon or simplifying a given pattern.

   A *rhythmic variation* is one which draws its substance

from a rational manipulation of the time-values of a rhythmic motive.

VERTICAL   1) Term used to describe all elements superposed vertically on the score and which are, therefore, heard simultaneously.

2) In polyphony, *vertical writing* tends to absorb the linearity of the different parts and favor massive harmonic effects.

WHOLE TONE OR WHOLE STEP   The largest diatonic division in the octave: there is a whole tone between C and D.

Sources

Barraqué, Jean. *Claude Debussy* (unpublished); *Notes* (unpublished); "Des Goûts et des Couleurs" in *Domaine Musical*, No. 1 (Julliard, Paris, 1954).

Berg, Alban. *Écrits*, translated and annotated by Henri Pousseur (Éditions du Rocher, Monaco).

Boulez, Pierre. "Eventuellement," in *La Revue Musicale* (April, 1952, Richard Masse, Paris). "Auprès et au Loin," in *La Musique et ses Problèmes Contemporains*, Cahiers de la Compagnie Renaud-Barrault (Paris, 1954). "Probabilités Critiques du Compositeur," in *Domaine Musical*, No. 1 (Julliard, Paris, 1954). "Aléa," in *La Nouvelle Revue Française* (Gallimard, Paris, November, 1957).

Deutsch, Max. "Arnold Schönberg," in *La Vie Musicale* (Revue Internationale de Musique, Paris, September, 1951).

Eimert and Stockhausen, eds. *Die Reihe I: Electronic Music* (Theodore Presser, 1958).

Fano, Michel. "Aspect de la Musique Contemporaine," *Le Point* (Mulhouse, March, 1954). *Wozzeck ou le Nouvel Opéra* (in collaboration with P. J. Jouve: Plon, 1952). *Berg et Webern* (unpublished).

Goléa, Antoine. *Rencontres avec Pierre Boulez* (Julliard, Paris, 1958).

Leibowitz, René. *Schoenberg and his School* (Philosophical Lib., New York, 1949). *Introduction à la Musique de Douze Sons* (l'Arche, Paris, 1948).

241

Messiaen, Olivier. *Technique de mon Langage Musical* (Leduc, Paris, 1942). "Lecture in Brussels" (Leduc, Paris, 1959).

Schloezer, Boris de, and Scriabine, Marina. *Problèmes de la Musique Moderne* (Éditions de Minuit, Paris, 1959).

Souvtchinsky, Pierre. *Musique Russe* (includes an article by Pierre Boulez, "Strawinsky Demeure": Presses Universitaires de France, Paris, 1953). "A Propos d'un Retard," in *La Musique et ses Problèmes Contemporains* (Julliard, Paris, 1954).

Stravinsky, Igor F., and Craft, Robert. *Conversations with Igor Stravinsky* (Doubleday, New York, 1959).

Stuckenschmidt, H. H. *Schoenberg* (Grove Press, New York, 1960).

A Selective Discography

BARRAQUÉ, JEAN
  Séquence; Ethel Semser, soprano; ensemble cond. Rudolf Albert. *Sonata;* Yvonne Loriod, piano; Véga C–30–A–180.*
  Étude. Barclay 89.005.*

BARTÓK, BÉLA
  Concerto for Orchestra; Chicago Symphony cond. Fritz Reiner. Victor LM–1934. [G.B.: Berlin RIAS Orch. cond. Ferenc Fricsay. DGM 18377.]
  Piano Concerto No. 1; Leonid Hambro, piano; Zimbler Sinfonietta cond. Robert Mann. Bartók 313.
  Piano Concertos Nos. 2 & 3; Edith Farnadi, piano; Vienna State Opera Orch. cond. Hermann Scherchen. Same coupling; Gyorgy Sandor, piano, Vienna Pro Musica cond. Michael Gielen. Vox PL–11490 [G.B.: same; stereo STPL 11490].
  Violin Concerto; Isaac Stern, violin, New York Philharmonic cond. Leonard Bernstein. Columbia ML–5283 [G.B.: Fontana CFL 1031; stereo SCFL 106]. Same; Tibor Varga, violin; Berlin Philharmonic cond. Ferenc Fricsay. Decca 9545 [G.B.: Deutsche Grammophon DGM 18006].
  Music for Strings, Percussion, and Celesta; Chicago Symphony

---

* Records released only on European labels. American and British releases added with the assistance of Mr. James Lyons and Mr. Gunther Schuller. [British releases in brackets.]

cond. Fritz Reiner. Victor LM–2374. Same; Chicago Symphony cond. R. Kubelik. Mercury 50001. [G.B.: Berlin RIAS Orch. cond. Ferenc Fricsay. DGXX 18493.]

String Quartets, Nos. 1–6; Fine Arts Quartet. Concert-Disc 1207/9. Same coupling; Juilliard Quartet. Columbia ML–4278/80 [G.B.: Philips ABL 3064, 3093, 3112].

BERG, ALBAN

Altenberg Lieder; Bethany Beardslee, soprano; Columbia Symphony cond. Robert Craft. Columbia ML–5428 (stereo: MS-6103).

Concerto for Violin and Orchestra; Louis Krasner, violin; Cleveland Orch. cond. Artur Rodzinski. Columbia ML–4857. [G.B.: Ivry Gitlis, violin, Vienna Pro Musica cond. Strickland. P.L. 10760.]

Lulu; Ilona Steingruber, Otto Wiener; Vienna Symphony cond. Herbert Häfner. Columbia SL–121.

Quartet, op. 3; Juilliard Quartet. Columbia ML–4737. Same; New Music Quartet. Bartók 906.

Sonata for Piano, op. 1; Glenn Gould, piano. Columbia ML–5336.

Three Pieces for Orchestra; Südwestdeutsches Orchester cond. Hans Rosbaud. Westminster XWN–18807.

Wozzeck; Eileen Farrell, Mack Harrell; New York Philharmonic cond. Dimitri Mitropoulos. Columbia SL–118.

Chamber Concerto; Charlotte Zelka, piano; Ivry Gitlis, violin; ensemble cond. Harold Byrns. Vox PL–8660. [G.B.: J. Monod, piano; R. Charmy, violin; Ensemble cond. René Liebowitz. Felsted RL 89004.]

BERIO, LUCIANO

Serenata I; ensemble cond. Pierre Boulez. Véga C–30–A–139.*

BOULEZ, PIERRE

Le Marteau sans Maître; Marie-Thérèse Cahn, contralto; ensemble cond. the composer. Westminster XWN–18746. Same; Marjorie MacKay, alto; ensemble cond. Robert Craft. Columbia ML–5275.

Sonatine; David Tudor, piano; Gazzeloni, flute. Véga C–30–A–139.*

Structures; Aloys and Alfons Kontarsky, pianos. Véga C–30–A–278.*

Etude II; Barclay 89.005.*

CAGE, JOHN

The 25-year Retrospective Concert (Recorded in actual performance at Town Hall May 15, 1958): *Six Short Inventions for Seven Instruments; Construction in Metal; Imaginary Landscape No. 1; The Wonderful Widow of Eighteen Springs; She Is Asleep; Sonatas I–VIII; First Interlude; Second Interlude; Music for Carillon; Williams Mix; Concert for Piano and Orchestra;* John Cage, piano; David Tudor, piano and electric carillon; Maro Ajemian, piano; Arline Carmen, contralto; Manhattan Percussion Ensemble; orchestra cond. Merce Cunningham. Available from George Avakian, 10 West 33rd Street, New York 1, N.Y.

Indeterminacy; John Cage, reader; David Tudor, piano, etc. Folkways FT–3704.

EIMERT, HERBERT

Einführung; Etüde über Tongemische; Fünf Stücke; Glockenspiel; Elektronische Realisation des WDR Köln. Deutsche Grammophon LP–16132.*

HENZE, HANS WERNER

Concerto per il Marigny; ensemble cond. Rudolf Albert. Véga C–30–A–180.*

Five Neapolitan Songs; Dietrich Fischer-Dieskau, baritone; Berlin Philharmonic cond. Richard Kraus. Deutsche Grammophon LPM–18406 [G.B.: same].*

KŘENEK, ERNST

Spiritus intelligentiae sanctus; Pfingsoratorium für Singstimmen und elektronische Klänge—1. Abteilung; Käthe Möller-Siepermann, soprano; Martin Häusler, tenor; Ernst Křenek, narrator; Elektronische Realisation des WDR Köln. Deutsche Grammophon LP–16134.*

MESSIAEN, OLIVIER

Études de Rythme (*Ile de Feu I & II, Mode de Valeurs et d'Intensités, Neumes Rythmiques*); Paul Jacobs, piano. Barclay 89.005.*

Oiseaux Exotiques; Yvonne Loriod, piano; ensemble cond. Rudolf Albert. Westminster XWN–18746.

Cantéyodjayà; Yvonne Loriod, piano. Boîte à Musique LD–050.*

The Complete Organ Works; O. Messiaen, organ, Ducretet 260–C–074/081.*

Trois Petites Liturgies de la Présence Divine; Yvonne Loriod, piano; J. Loriod, Martenot; ensemble cond. Marcel Couraud. Ducretet 270–C–075.*

Vingt Regards sur l'Enfant Jésus; Yvonne Loriod, piano. Westminster 18469/70.

NONO, LUIGI

Incontri; cond. Pierre Boulez. Vèga C–30–A–66.*

PHILIPPOT, MICHEL

Ambiance I; Boîte à Musique Ex–241.*

Étude; Ducretet-Thomson DTL–93121.*

POUSSEUR, HENRI

Mobile; Aloys and Alfons Kontarsky, pianos. Véga C–30–A–278.*

SCHÖNBERG, ARNOLD

Canon for String Quartet; Herzgewaechse, op. 20; The New Classicism (Cantata); Piano Pieces, op. 33a–b; Marni Nixon, soprano; ensemble cond. Robert Craft. Columbia ML–5099.

Chamber Symphony, op. 9; SW German Radio Symphony cond. Jascha Horenstein. Vox PL–10460 [G.B.: same].

Chamber Symphony, op. 38; Vienna Symphony cond. Herbert Häfner. Columbia ML–4664.

Piano Concerto; Alfred Brendel, piano; SW German Radio Symphony cond. Michael Gielen. Vox PL–10530 [G.P.: same].

Violin Concerto; Louis Krasner, violin; New York Philharmonic cond. Dimitri Mitropoulos. Columbia ML–4857.

Same; Heinrich Marschner, violin; SW German Radio Symphony cond. Michael Gielen. Vox 10530 [G.B.: PL 10530].

Kol Nidre, op. 39; Hans Jaray, narrator; Academie Chamber Chorus; Vienna Symphony cond. Hans Swarowsky. Columbia ML–4664.

Moses und Aron; Hans Herbert Fiedler, speaker; Helmut Krebs, Ilona Steingruber, singers; Norddeutscher Rundfunk cond. Hans Rosbaud. Columbia K3L–241.

Piano Music (complete); Edward Steurmann, piano. Columbia ML–5216.

Five Pieces for Orchestra, op. 16; Columbia Symphony cond. Robert Craft. Columbia ML–5428. Same; Chicago Symphony cond. R. Kubelik. Mercury 50024.

Pierrot Lunaire; Ethel Semser, soprano; Virtuoso Ensemble cond. René Liebowitz. Westminster XWN–18143 [G.B.: Argo RG54]. Same; Stiedry-Wagner, soloist; Schönberg Orchestra cond. by composer. Col. ML–4471.

String Quartets (complete); The Juilliard Quartet. Columbia SL–188.

Wind Quintet, op. 26; Philadelphia Woodwind Ensemble. Columbia ML–5217.

Survivor from Warsaw; Hans Jaray, narrator; Academie Chamber Chorus; Vienna Symphony cond. Hans Swarowsky. Columbia ML–4664.

Variations for Orchestra, op. 31; Serenade for Baritone and Septet, op. 24; Four Pieces, op. 27; Canon: The Parting of the Ways, op. 28, no. 1; Sam van Ducen, bass; ensembles cond. Robert Craft. Columbia ML–5244.

SCHULLER, GUNTHER

String Quartet; Walden Quartet. UI–CRS 5 (Available through the University of Illinois Bookstore).

Seven Studies on Themes of Paul Klee; Minneapolis Symphony Orchestra cond. Antal Dorati. Mercury (to be released).

STOCKHAUSEN, KARLHEINZ

Studie I; Studie II; Gesang der Jünglinge I; Elektronische Realisation des WDR Köln. Deutsche Grammophon LP–16133.*

Nr. 5 Zeitmasse; ensemble cond. Robert Craft. Columbia ML–5275.

Klavierstück VI; David Tudor, piano. Véga C–30–A–278.*

Kontrapunkte; ensemble cond. Pierre Boulez. Véga C–30–A–66.*

STRAVINSKY, IGOR

Agon; Canticum Sacrum; Soloists; Los Angeles Festival Symphony cond. the composer. Columbia ML–5215. Same; Südwestdeutsches Orchester cond. Rosbaud. Westminster 18807.

Apollon Musagète; Renard; Orch. Suisse Romande cond. Ernest Ansermet. London CM–9152 [G.B.: Decca LXT 5169].

Le Baiser de la fée (complete); Soloists; Cleveland Orch. cond. the composer. Columbia ML–5102.

Cantata (1952); Symphony in C; Jennie Tourel, mezzo; Hugues Cuénod, tenor; New York Concert Choir; Cleveland Orch. cond. the composer. Columbia ML–4899.

Capriccio; Concerto for Two Solo Pianos; Charlotte Zelka, Alfred Brendel, pianos; SW German Radio Symphony cond. Harold Byrns. Vox PL–10660 [G.B.: same].

Violin Concerto; Ivry Gitlis, violin; Concerts Colonne Orch. cond. Harold Byrns. Vox PL–10760 [G.B.: same].

Concerto Grosso in D; Boston Orch. cond. Willis Page. Cook 1062.

The Firebird (complete); London Symphony cond. Antal Dorati. Mercury MG–50226 [G.B.: MMA 11089; stereo AMS 16038].

The Firebird Suite; Berlin Radio Symphony cond. Lorin Maazel. Decca 9978 [G.B.: Deutsche Grammophon DGM 18498; stereo SLPM 138006].

Fireworks; Ode; Russian Maiden's Song; Norwegian Moods; Circus Polka; New York Philharmonic cond. the composer. Columbia ML–4398.

L'Histoire du Soldat (suite); Octet; Symphonies of Wind Instruments; NW German Radio Orch. cond. the composer. Columbia ML–4964.

Oedipus Rex; Soloists; Cologne Radio Symphony & Chorus cond. the composer. Columbia ML–4644 [G.B.: Philips ABL 3054].

Perséphone; Soloists; New York Philharmonic cond. the composer. Columbia ML–5196.

Petrouchka (complete); Philharmonic Orch. cond. Efrem Kurtz. Angel 35553 [G.B.: Philips APL 1503]; Same; Minneapolis Symphony cond. Antal Dorati. Mercury MG–50216.

Pulcinella (complete); Soloists, Cleveland Orch. cond. the composer. Columbia ML–4830.

The Rake's Progress (complete); Soloists, Metropolitan Opera Orch. cond. the composer. Columbia SL–125 [G.B.: Philips ABL 3055–7].

Le Sacre du Printemps; New York Philharmonic cond. Leonard Bernstein. Columbia ML–5277 [G.B.: Philips ABL 3268]. Same; Paris Conservatory Orch. cond. Pierre Monteux. Victor LM 2085 [G.B.: RCA RB 16007; stereo SB 2005].

Septet (1953); chamber group cond. the composer. Columbia ML–5107.

Song of the Nightingale (1919); Chicago Symphony cond. Fritz Reiner. Victor LM–2150. Same; Berlin Radio Symphony cond. Lorin Maazel. Decca 9978. [G.B.: Deutsche Grammophon DGM 18498; stereo SLPM 138006.]

Symphony of Psalms; French National Radio Chorus and Orch. cond. Jascha Horenstein. Angel 35101. [G.B.: (with *L'Histoire du Soldat suite*) CBS Symphony cond. the composer. Philips ABL 3065.]

Symphony in Three Movements; New York Philharmonic cond. the composer. Columbia ML–4129.

Threni (id est Lamentationes Jeremiae Prophetae); Beardslee, Krebs, Lewis, Wainner, Morgan, Oliver, soloists; Schola Cantorum, Columbia Symphony Orchestra cond. Stravinsky. Columbia ML–5383.

VARÈSE, EDGAR

Densité; René le Roy, flute. EMS–401.

Intégrales; Ionisation; Octandre; Juilliard Percussion Orchestra cond. Frederick Waldman. EMS–401.

WEBERN, ANTON

The Complete Works, opp. 1–31; *Piano Quintet* (1906, ed. Monod); Orch. of *Ricercar* from Bach's *Musical Offering;* Soloists and ensembles cond. Robert Craft. Columbia K4L–232 [G.B.: LO 9414–7].

Six Pieces for Orchestra, op. 6; Südwestdeutsches Orchester cond. Rosbaud. Westminster 18657.

Variations, op. 27; Paul Jacobs, piano. *Lieder, opp. 3, 23;* Ethel Semser, sopr.; Jacobs, piano. Barclay 89.005.*

Index